THE BENCHMARKING BOOK

Michael J. Spendolini

amacom

American Management Association

New York • Atlanta • Boston • Chicago • Kansas City • San Francisco • Washington, D.C.
Brussels • Toronto • Mexico City

This publication is designed to provide accurate and authoritative
information in regard to the subject matter covered. It is sold with the
understanding that the publisher is not engaged in rendering legal,
accounting, or other professional service. If legal advice or other
expert assistance is required, the services of a competent professional
person should be sought.

Library of Congress Cataloging-in-Publication Data

Spendolini, Michael J.
  The benchmarking book / Michael J. Spendolini.
     p.   cm.
  Includes index.
  ISBN 0-8144-5077-6 (hardcover)
  1. Total quality management. I. Title.
HD62.15.S65   1992
658.5'62—dc20   91-48024
                                              CIP

Printing number

10 9 8 7 6 5 4 3

To
my
parents,
Nix and **Flo**

Contents

Preface

In the spring of 1991 I attended a two-day symposium on benchmarking that was held in northern California. This symposium was noteworthy in that it was one of the first of its kind to be conducted on such a scale. There were impressive speakers from companies such as Xerox, Cadillac, Abbott Labs, and NCR. There were keynote speakers, breakout sessions, panels, displays—the whole array of conference events. Although the subject of benchmarking was beginning to appear on the agendas of conferences and symposia that focused on total quality management or the Malcolm Baldrige Award, this particular conference demonstrated the emergence of benchmarking as a subject that was worthy of its own agenda.

I was excited about attending this symposium. At the time, I was offering training and consulting services on the subject of benchmarking. This meeting promised to be a terrific opportunity to connect with other trainers, consultants, and potential clients. It was also an opportunity to gauge state-of-the-art benchmarking practices as presented by some well-known organizations having considerable experience with the process. It was an exciting agenda, and, for the most part, the sponsors delivered an excellent program. The people who attended seemed to be in good spirits before, during, and after the event.

I attended the conference to observe and listen to what the conference attendees had to say as much as to hear what the conference presenters had to offer. It didn't take long to notice that the conference audience was obviously split into two categories. The first category consisted of those people whose knowledge of benchmarking was extremely limited. Perhaps they had read an article on the subject or had run across the term in the Baldrige award guidelines or had attended a lecture at one of the quality symposia. They were attending this conference to find out what benchmarking was all about and how the process might fit in to their organizations. For the most part, these attendees were fairly quiet. They would occasionally ask a question for clarification, but mostly they just listened. The second category of attendees was already committed to using (or attempting to use) the process. In some cases, their organizations had already begun to introduce the process and they were gearing up for their first benchmarking projects. Others already had some experience with the process and were attending to broaden their perspective, learn something from the experts, and begin the process of networking with other benchmarkers. Another subset of this group were those individuals who had the task of implementing, training, or managing the benchmarking process in their organizations. Their questions tended to be specific and were focused, to a large extent, on implementation issues.

The presenters' messages were well structured and easy for the audience to follow. Virtually all the presenters focused on the benchmarking process as it was used in their organizations, and they illustrated their own processes with examples. They also added some interesting comments concerning lessons learned from their experiences. These lessons were usually learned the hard way after encountering some sort of process problem. Whenever they offered a suggestion based on these lessons, I noticed that the audience began taking copious notes.

During day one of the conference, the audience's comments about the presentations were positive and optimistic. A few outrageous stories that had been presented circulated among the attendees. As the conference entered its second day, the comments and reactions of the conference attendees became far more interesting to me than the presentations themselves. I found myself taking copious notes during break times.

Three types of comments were beginning to be heard with some regularity. First, as day two wore on, people began to note that the presentations were repetitious. The stories, models, and lessons were all beginning to sound alike. This was a good news–bad news reaction: The good news was that the messages from experienced benchmarkers seemed to be consistent—there were no exotic versions of benchmarking to complicate their understanding; the bad news was simply the boredom factor.

A second type of comment focused on the fact that every benchmarking model that was presented over the course of the two days was different. Although they were all similar in appearance and intent, the fact remained that no two models were exactly alike. The audience was asking, "Do we all have to make up our own models?" For individuals who were looking for some direction and a clear message regarding the correct approach, the variety of models raised a number of questions. The good news was that all the models seemed to share a generic core; the bad news was that no one had offered the audience a presentation on these common elements.

The third type of comment was the most interesting to me. Many attendees felt that they had received a lot of information about the benchmarking experiences of each organization represented. However, they were leaving the conference without a clear set of directions on exactly what they had to do to establish benchmarking in their own organizations. Although no one had expected to receive a cookbook description of every possible action that should be considered, these people felt that not enough time had been dedicated to the benchmarking start-up experience.

Having an empirical mind (sometimes a shortcoming rather than an advantage), I recorded my observations from the conference and looked for an opportunity to test my conclusions. I got my chance twice within the next three months. Two similar conferences sponsored by two different organizations were held on benchmarking; both were scheduled for two days and each had approximately 150 participants. The agendas for the two conferences were virtually identical to that of the first one I had attended. This time, however, I not only listened to the comments of the conference attendees, I also conducted mini-interviews whenever an opportunity presented itself. I asked fairly open-ended questions: What important lessons are you taking away from this seminar? What elements of the benchmarking process do you think should be covered in more detail? What are your immediate challenges as a novice benchmarker? Where do you and your organization go from here? A lot of people asked me if I was a reporter.

The responses from the participants at these two conferences were the same as the comments I had heard at the first conference. And although there were one or two presenters at these later conferences who did a good job of discussing the generic elements of the benchmarking process, they represented a small portion of the overall agenda.

The experience of attending these meetings and listening to the needs of the benchmarking audience gave me the momentum I needed to write this book. This book presents a generic model of benchmarking that is appropriate for any organization, whether it be large or small, product- or service-oriented, public or private, even domestic or foreign. I propose a set of actions that an individual, group, or organization can take to establish its own benchmarking process. It is a hands-on approach that is light on the theoretical and heavy on the practical. Finally, this book summarizes the lessons learned from those companies that have experience with the benchmarking process. Readers are encouraged to take the advice of those companies and to consider the benchmarking don'ts as much as the benchmarking do's.

The methodology I chose to collect information for the book was basic. During the past several years, I have worked with dozens of companies, helping them use the benchmarking process to improve their businesses and, more importantly, helping them establish their own internal benchmarking processes and support capabilities. During that time, I observed some organizations adopt aggressive benchmarking policies, position adequate resources to ensure success, and develop a healthy outlook on benchmarking and its relationship to organizational philosophy. On the down side, I also saw benchmarking treated as just another program and watched it fade prematurely because of ambivalence or lack of understanding or support.

My intent was to focus my attention on only the best benchmarking companies and to extract those elements of their programs and processes that helped make them successful benchmarkers. I also wanted to note those problems and symptoms that typified some of the process failures and frustrations. With this goal in mind, I proceeded to develop a plan that would help me to benchmark the benchmarkers.

I first established a list of companies that had established a reputation for "best-practices" benchmarking. I started with my previous employer, Xerox, and continued to trace the spread of the process through other organizations that had learned from the Xerox experience. As I identified each benchmarking organization, I interviewed benchmarking specialists and employees who had experience with the process and who had worked to improve their benchmarking practices and capabilities. From these interviews I developed the framework for a generic model of benchmarking and summarized the lessons learned from those people and their companies.

I initially identified fifty-seven companies as possible "best-practices" candidates (the list could have been much larger). Each of these companies had been nominated for consideration by expert sources including consultants, benchmarking specialists from experienced benchmarking companies such as Xerox and AT&T, members of associations that had established benchmarking networks (e.g., the American Productivity and Quality Center [APQC], The Conference Board), articles in the general business press, and benchmarking conference organizers. I developed a set of questions regarding the approach, deployment, and results of the benchmarking process and conducted preliminary screening interviews with representatives of the fifty-seven companies. In order to progress to the next phase of the interview process, an organization had to demonstrate the existence and use of a formal benchmarking process; it had to have completed several iterations of the benchmarking process; and it had to be willing to share its findings with me over the telephone (there were no refusals). After this initial screening phase, I reduced my list to twenty-four companies for further interviews and analysis. Why these twenty-four? First, they met the criteria I just mentioned. More important, these organizations had spent a considerable amount of time developing their benchmarking concepts. They were dedicated to the process, as evidenced by their commitment of resources. They took a long-term view of benchmarking as a process that would be a major factor in helping them achieve their quality objectives. They also did a good job of integrating benchmarking into the day-to-day activities of their companies and tying benchmarking to their "bottom lines."

As I developed the generic benchmarking model that would serve as the basis for this book, I constantly reviewed my direction and much of the material with many of the individual benchmarking experts who participated in the interviews. Their feedback and suggestions were invaluable as a process check and for the additional insights and stories they shared with me.

The result of this effort is the generic benchmarking process model presented in this book. My intent was not to load page after page with specific examples from each company that was interviewed but, rather, to distill the lessons learned from the best-practices benchmarking companies and use examples to illustrate key points.

This book will be useful to those of you who are just beginning to understand the benchmarking process. There are enough definitions and examples to give you a basic orientation. If you are already starting to apply the process in your organization, this book offers an opportunity to learn from some of the most experienced benchmarkers and to broaden your perspective and possibly your approach. If you are an experienced benchmarker, this book presents an opportunity to conduct a process audit of your benchmarking activities. Some of the ideas and recommendations discussed in the book might stimulate ideas that will help you to continually improve your benchmarking process.

This project was an interesting, engaging, and fun undertaking. Benchmarking the benchmarkers redefined my definition of the term *learning experience*. For those of you who are novice benchmarkers, the process may seem like a lot of work and not a lot of fun, but take heart. As you gain experience with the process, many of the preparatory steps and technicalities become routine. What's left is the process of discovery and learning, of developing networks of interesting people, of bringing new ideas into your own work and organization. It can be a very rewarding experience for people who are motivated to listen and learn.

Acknowledgments

I would like to acknowledge the help and support of the people who helped me with my work on this book.

I would like to thank Edward Selig, senior program director for the American Management Association, who helped me to develop the design of the benchmarking course, which ultimately led to the writing of this book. Ed has a knack for getting people excited about a good idea, and his techniques of persuasion worked wonders for me. I would also like to thank Myles Thompson, my AMACOM acquisitions editor, who supported my writing efforts and left many motivational messages on my answering machine during the course of production. Ed and Myles were not only helpful as managers and editors of my work, they were also helpful as friends. I would also like to thank Kate Pferdner, who managed the editing process, for her patience and persistence.

I would like to thank Brien Lowenthal and Neil Thompson of The Benchmark Partners in Oak Brook, Illinois, for their ideas and support during the production of the book. Both Brien and Neil have been working with me to help organizations implement the benchmarking process, and our emphasis has been on the need to "do it right the first time." Our hope is that this book will help organizations to do just that.

Finally, I owe a great deal to the dedicated quality specialists, benchmarking experts, managers, and employees of the following organizations, who gave of their time, their interest, and their insights to make this book possible:

- Alcoa
- Allied Signal
- AT&T
- Bell Atlantic
- Boeing
- Caterpillar
- Digital Equipment
  Corporation
- Eastman Kodak
- E. I. Du Pont de Nemours &
  Co., Inc.
- Florida Power & Light
- Hewlett-Packard
- Hughes Aircraft
- IBM
- John Deere
- Johnson & Johnson
- L. L. Bean
- Milliken
- Motorola
- NCR
- Procter & Gamble
- Square D
- 3M
- Wallace
- Weyerhaeuser
- Xerox

Part One

Benchmarking Basics

1

The Benchmarking Concept

The history of benchmarking as we know it today is relatively brief. In 1982 I went to Rochester, New York, to attend a meeting of Xerox Corporation's training and organizational development specialists. The term *competitive benchmarking* was used in a discussion of the immense performance gap that Xerox had identified in relation to its competitors. Specific standards of measurement, or metrics, in areas such as production costs, cycle time, overhead costs, retail selling prices, and product features were identified, and the performance of Xerox was ranked in relation to that of its chief market rivals for those metrics. The news was not good. Those in attendance were not happy with the information we had reviewed. However, most were impressed with the process that was used to identify key metrics, gather information about other companies, and present the findings in a particularly interesting context.

The term *competitive benchmarking* was new to most of us, and after I returned to my office in California, I found that the term was new to just about everyone I knew in the training and development field. When I explained the concept and purpose of benchmarking, the first reaction was usually one of recognition of the process as a type of competitive intelligence gathering. But as I continued to explain the term, two facets of benchmarking caught people's attention. First, benchmarking was a process that could be used to understand not only one's competitors but *any* organization—competitor or noncompetitor, large or small, public or private, foreign or domestic. The key is to isolate common metrics in like functions (e.g., manufacturing, engineering, marketing, finance) and compare one's own business practices with those of organizations that have established themselves as leaders or innovators in that specific business function. The idea of generic excellence makes this possible. If, for example, one accepts the fact that a particular activity, such as billing, is a common practice in practically any organization, then there should also exist some generic billing practices that can be observed and measured in any organization. In addition, if one can investigate the billing practices of organizations that have established an excellent reputation in the practice of billing, then one might be able to compare those generic billing practices to the practices in one's own organization. One might even learn something from the other company regarding its excellent billing practices. This idea of studying the business practices of other organizations did not shock or disturb anyone. What did cause people to react was the fact that this investigation could be conducted on such a systematic and extensive basis.

A second facet of benchmarking also caused people to take note. At that time, competitive intelligence gathering traditionally focused almost entirely on measuring outcomes or finished products. Concepts such as reverse engineering or side-by-side product comparisons were easy to understand. With benchmarking, the focus extended beyond the scope of the finished product or service to concentrate extensively on *process* issues. The emphasis was not only on *what* another organization produced, but also on *how* the product or service was designed, manufactured, marketed, and serviced. In fact, an organization might be considered for investigation based on process excellence, not just product or service excellence. This was a radical concept to many people. *Process*, after all, was a term that implied complexity and intimate inner workings. Even the processes within one's own organization are often shrouded in mystery and propriety. How could anyone even bring up the subject of a process investigation with an *outsider*? Besides, in order to really understand process, one had to establish a close link with the other organization. Simply examining a product or service from a distance would not provide the level of detail necessary to truly understand an organization's actions. Benchmarking was somehow more intimate than traditional competitive intelligence gathering. In fact, there was an openness and a spirit of (dare it be said) cooperation between organizations that might be competitors in the marketplace. I knew then that the paradigm of information gathering and organizational analysis had shifted significantly.

Xerox continued to develop the concept of competitive benchmarking through the 1980s, establishing formal training on the subject and introducing the concept to others via customers, suppliers, articles written by Xerox employees, and contacts in professional associations. Other companies, such as GTE, began to use the term as early as 1983, but it wasn't until the late 1980s that *benchmarking* really hit its stride. Up until that time, the number of articles on the subject totaled less than thirty, and there were few (if any) experts on the practice of benchmarking in either the consulting or academic ranks. Two significant events changed all that.

One was the introduction of the Malcolm Baldrige National Quality Award. The Malcolm Baldrige National Quality Improvement Act of 1987, Public Law 100-107, was signed by President Reagan on August 20, 1987, and established an annual U.S. National Quality Award. The stated purposes of the award were to promote quality awareness, to recognize quality achievements in U.S. companies, and to publicize successful quality strategies. The award criteria consist of seven categories, each of which includes specific areas to address that identify key quality activities and processes that are advocated by the award committee.

One issue raised by the Baldrige award is that of external comparisons. Users of the criteria are encouraged to consider the nature and effectiveness of their quality practices and results in relation to those of other organizations that are referred to simply as "best-in-class" or "world-class" (the Baldrige consortium does not venture to identify these organizations or how to locate them, but that's another story). Thus, the users of the criteria are explicitly urged to compare their quality practices not only with competitors but with any organization that has achieved notable excellence in process or results. The only drawback of this recommendation was that the guidelines did not specify any method for making these comparisons—that is, they didn't until 1991. When the 1991 award application and guidelines were published, an important addition was made to the Baldrige lexicon. Under the category "Information and Analysis," item 2.2 was entitled "Competitive Comparisons and Benchmarks." The description of this item reads, "Describe the company's approach to selecting quality-related competitive comparisons and world-class benchmarks to support quality planning, evaluation, and improvement." This strong emphasis on benchmarking was repeated five more times within the 1991 guidelines in areas such as assessing continuous improvement efforts, product and service quality results, supplier quality results, and the determination of customer satisfaction.

The emphasis on process and results comparisons stimulated an unprecedented interest in the subject of benchmarking; organizations serious about using the Baldrige guidelines or applying for the award were motivated to learn about the subject and to discover any resources that might be available to help them benchmark properly. The problem was that there weren't many explicit guidelines, rules, models, or experts to help them understand and apply benchmarking to their organizations.

The other significant event that I mentioned had occurred two years earlier, in 1989. Robert Camp, a Xerox logistics expert and engineer, wrote *Benchmarking: The Search for Industry Best Practices That Lead to Superior Performance*, in which he describes in detail his seven years of benchmarking activities within Xerox. The book was framed around the Xerox ten-step benchmarking process, which he had helped design and launch. Camp's book included specific examples of benchmarking in the areas of logistics and distribution, which provided the reader with tangible examples of the process in use and the kinds of results that could be achieved. The Camp book was the first detailed description of benchmarking in action that was available to the general business audience, and it quickly became a best-seller among those who were responsible for investigating or implementing benchmarking in their organizations.

The publication of the Camp book could not have been more timely, for in 1989 Xerox Corporation (Business Products and Systems Division) was one of only two Baldrige award recipients for that year (only three companies had been named winners in the prior, inaugural year). Thus, as would become the case for every Baldrige winner, Xerox was besieged with requests for information about its quality process and practices. In fact, one of the stated responsibilities of Baldrige award winners is to share information on quality strategies and encourage other companies to raise their quality standards. Xerox now had an eager audience that was curious to understand the company's success with its "Leadership Through Quality" strategy.

Since the early 1980s, Xerox had traditionally positioned its quality strategy as a three-legged stool, and one of those legs was—you guessed it!—benchmarking. Thus, as hundreds, and even thousands, of people studied the Xerox quality process and heard the Xerox quality message, it became clear that benchmarking was one of the keys to its success. The fact that the Camp book was already available made it an instant success. In fact, that book was probably the first in-depth source of benchmarking information for the vast majority of its readers.

One would have thought that by 1991 other significant books or training programs would have been written to expand the available perspective on benchmarking. The reality, however, was that by 1991 the Camp book was still the only one of its kind, and only a few consulting companies had developed programs to help explain and implement benchmarking programs. Articles that appeared in the general business and trade publications continued to repeat the same examples over and over again to "position" benchmarking for their readers. So though interest in benchmarking was at an all-time high, information about the subject, expecially hands-on or how-to references, was still scarce.

This lack of information, models, examples, and guidelines becomes apparent when one examines the benchmarking processes in place today. Many if not most benchmarking processes can trace their genealogy directly to the Xerox model of the early 1980s or to one or two approaches that originated from a few consulting companies. Although the core of these benchmarking approaches is similar, most of the organizations using the process have tailored their definitions and approaches to conform to existing models or programs in their environments. Thus, in addition to the Xerox ten-step benchmarking process, there is the AT&T nine-step process, the Alcoa six-step process, the IBM five-phase/fourteen-step process, the DEC four-phase process, and so on. An outsider new to benchmarking would be hard-pressed to produce a definition of the benchmarking process that would conform to more than a few of the models that exist out in the real world of benchmarking.

Toward a Definition of Benchmarking

Sometimes definitions seem like necessary evils, which is one reason that many people don't like them. As soon as a definition is proposed, it seems that people immediately take exception to it; the more a definition is positioned as *the* definition or embellished with testimonials, the more people attempt to shoot holes in it. Defining benchmarking at this stage in its life seems to be a lose-lose proposition. Because *benchmarking* as a term has been tweaked and customized by so many organizations, attempting to define it might serve to isolate or irritate those very organizations that have attempted to work with the process on a formal basis. They already have their own definitions of benchmarking and might be critical of any other. On the other hand, those new to the subject of benchmarking might take note of a new definition of benchmarking and, upon contrasting it with other definitions on the market, tweak and customize the definition to suit their own purposes anyway.

I decided to take an empirical approach to the definition of benchmarking in order to position it in light of the variety of definitions that already existed. In mid-1991, I took a poll of organizations that had established a reputation for using a formal process of benchmarking and producing satisfactory results through its use. I made my choice after examining several sources: articles on the subject, expert sources in several professional associations, contacts in some of the companies known as experienced benchmarkers, and consultants experienced in benchmarking. I sought out organizations regardless of their size, their product or service orientation, or their being public or private. On the basis of these criteria, I identified fifty-seven companies as the subjects of my investigation.

I called each of the fifty-seven companies and tried to locate its internal benchmarking experts. I then conducted a brief interview covering the organization's definition of benchmarking, use of any type of formal process, descriptions of "typical" benchmark applications, as well as information regarding benchmarking training, positioning of benchmarking in relation to other quality practices and tools, and a variety of other benchmarking issues. Of the fifty-seven companies I initially contacted, forty-nine had established some type of formal definition of benchmarking. Of these forty-nine definitions, forty-one consisted of variants of other definitions that the experts had been exposed to through their readings on the subject, consultant advice or training, or contact with companies such as Xerox.

The Benchmarking Menu

After collecting forty-nine definitions of benchmarking, I set out to investigate any patterns in the language. Most definitions were one or two sentences long, and there was the usual accompaniment of bullets, boxes, and arrows. There was also a definite pattern in the language used to describe benchmarking—a commonality in both the types of words used and their apparent intent. Now the challenge was to narrow down the list of words to develop a single definition that could serve as a generic baseline for the term. After many attempts I finally felt satisfied with my result. Then I decided to pilot test my definition with some colleagues and some of the benchmarking experts I had contacted earlier. What an ordeal! As predicted, everyone wanted to tweak the definition, add a few bullets, change just a few words. It was obvious that any definition I proposed would be challenged or changed in some way; there didn't seem to be any way to satisfy everyone.

Then I had an idea—an old word game in which sentences are formed by selecting words out of clusters of nouns, adjectives, verbs, and so on, and joining them together. It's like a menu where you choose one word from column A, one from column B, and so on. If I could isolate key word clusters I could create a menu that would allow anyone to construct a working definition that met his or her preferences while maintaining the definition's basic integrity. This approach also forces definers to think about the words in each cluster a little more carefully and involves them in the active creation of their own working definitions. I tried this approach with the same test group with excellent results. Virtually all of my sample group were able to reconstruct their own existing definitions of benchmarking, and a few played with the menu and created some interesting—and in some cases bizarre—spins on their definitions.

Exhibit 1-1 presents the benchmarking menu. The objective is to select one word or phrase from each of the nine boxes and create a definition of benchmarking. In some cases, you may select more than one item from a box to create a more comprehensive definition. Also note that at the bottom of most boxes is a blank space. If you want to add another word or phrase to any box based upon your own experience with benchmarking, simply add it and see how it fits. The following demonstration is one of the definitions of benchmarking that I constructed after my original survey of the forty-nine benchmarking companies with formal definitions. The box number of each word in the definition (in parentheses) is added to illustrate how I used the menu:

Benchmarking: A continuous(1), systematic(2) process(3) for evaluating(4) the products(5), services(5), and work processes(5) of organizations(6) that are recognized(7) as representing best practices(8) for the purpose of organizational improvement(9).

Exhibit 1-1. The benchmarking menu.

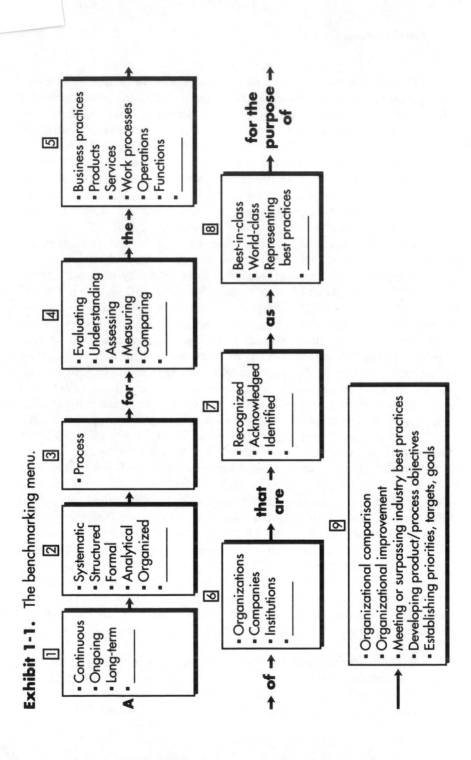

A

1
- Continuous
- Ongoing
- Long-term
- ___

2
- Systematic
- Structured
- Formal
- Analytical
- Organized
- ___

3
- Process

for

4
- Evaluating
- Understanding
- Assessing
- Measuring
- Comparing
- ___

the

5
- Business practices
- Products
- Services
- Work processes
- Operations
- Functions
- ___

of

6
- Organizations
- Companies
- Institutions
- ___

that are

7
- Recognized
- Acknowledged
- Identified
- ___

as

8
- Best-in-class
- World-class
- Representing best practices
- ___

for the purpose of

9
- Organizational comparison
- Organizational improvement
- Meeting or surpassing industry best practices
- Developing product/process objectives
- Establishing priorities, targets, goals

You can experiment with combinations of words to see which ones work for you. The only requirement is that you include at least one item from each of the nine boxes. Each box in Exhibit 1-1 was included for a purpose, and a definition of benchmarking should reflect consideration of each of the nine key elements. Let's review the nine word clusters and consider their implications.

Box 1 (continuous, ongoing, long-term). This cluster of words suggests that benchmarking is something that takes place over an extended period of time. It is not a short-term or a one-time activity. In order for benchmarking information to be meaningful, it must often be considered in a context that acknowledges organizational activity over time. Organizations that have successfully incorporated benchmarking have recognized that organizational behavior and performance are not static—they change over time. To simply benchmark the present on a one-time basis denies this dynamic assumption. The same holds true for understanding the activities of a benchmark partner. A "snapshot" measure of another organization does not accurately reflect the dynamic nature of its business strategies or outcomes.

Exhibit 1-2 illustrates the point. This graph reflects the activity of Organization A on a particular measure—research and development (R&D) spending as a percent of sales. This measure is graphed over a period of five years from 1990 to 1994, with 1992 designated as the present year. The same information is graphed for Organization B. Let's assume that Organization A is your organization and Organization B represents one of your closest competitors. If you simply collected benchmark information for the present time (i.e., 1992), what would that tell you? Note that in 1992 the level of R&D spending is almost identical for the two organizations. What conclusions could you reach from this fact? What decisions would you make?

Now consider an extension of the same information to include a historical period (1990 to 1991) and a projection of future R&D expenditures. Now what do the data indicate? Your organization (A) has established a relatively flat level of spending, while Organization B is on an accelerating curve. What questions are raised by this information? What types of follow-up questions or issues come to mind? Historical and future perspectives add a more dynamic dimension to the information. A continuous or ongoing perspective on benchmarking reinforces this type of thinking during the benchmarking process. "Snapshot" measures or short-term perspectives do not produce the most useful

Exhibit 1-2. R&D spending of Organizations A and B
(1990–1994).

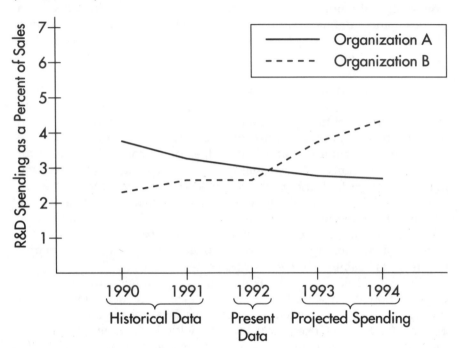

benchmarking results, whether one is examining one's own work processes or those of a competitor or model company.

Box 2 (systematic, structured, formal, analytical, organized). There
is a method to benchmarking. For most companies, this fact is demonstrated by the existence of some type of benchmarking process model
or flowchart that encourages a recommended set of actions in some
particular order. These models represent a consistent and expected
sequence that can be repeated by any member or organization, suggesting that benchmarking is not a loosely structured information-gathering
exercise. The advantages of having a certain level of formality and
structure become apparent when an organization expands the use of
benchmarking to a large number of employees. Employees do not have
to invent or tailor benchmarking to their particular needs or departmen-

tal language. There is consistency among organizational functions and locations as well as a common set of expectations regarding the realistic outcomes of benchmarking.

Box 3 (process). The idea that benchmarking is a process is a given. Virtually every definition of benchmarking emphasizes the idea that benchmarking involves a series of actions that define issues, problems, or opportunities; measures performance (both one's own and that of others); draws conclusions based on an analysis of the information collected; and stimulates organizational change and improvement. Whether one examines the Xerox ten-step benchmarking process, the Alcoa six-step process, the IBM fourteen-step process, or the AT&T nine-step process, the fact is that there is a significant emphasis on the *process* of benchmarking.

Box 4 (evaluating, understanding, assessing, measuring, comparing). Benchmarking is an investigative process—a process of inquiry. Note that all the words in this cluster denote action, not passivity. Benchmarking does not deliver answers. It is through the process of measuring, evaluating, comparing, and so on that one produces information that will add value to the quality of decision making. Benchmarking should be realistically positioned as an investigative process that produces information that helps people make decisions. Quite simply, benchmarking is a tool that helps people learn about themselves and others.

Box 5 (business practices, products, services, work processes, operations, functions). Benchmarking is not limited to any one facet of an organization's activities. Most definitions of benchmarking emphasize the fact that benchmarking is useful in understanding work processes as well as the finished products or services these processes produce. At first, benchmarking reminds some people of traditional definitions of competitive analysis, where the emphasis is on comparisons of finished products or services. The idea of considering business practices or processes that focus on *how* rather than on *what* is a difficult transition for many people to make. A broad perspective regarding the potential subjects of benchmarking was recommended by a benchmarking advocate at IBM. She said, "If something can be measured, it can be benchmarked—period!"

Box 6 (organizations, companies, institutions). The focus of benchmarking is not limited to competitive products, services, or practices. As the definition of benchmarking is expanded to include generic business processes, it becomes evident that benchmarking can be applied to any organization that produces similar outputs or engages in similar business practices. The specific type of organization as defined by industry, size, location, or ownership is not a limiting factor for most benchmarking analyses. For many who have not had experience with an organized benchmarking effort, the idea of examining the work processes of an organization very different from their own is difficult to accept. Most benchmarking organizations claim that it takes some actual benchmarking experience to increase one's comfort level with the process.

Throughout this book, I use the term *benchmark partners* to refer to the individuals and organizations that furnish information about best practices. Some individuals act as information brokers and direct you toward other sources of best-practices information. Others assist in your benchmarking activities such as training, process facilitation, and information gathering. Your partners are also employees of the organizations you are benchmarking. The word *partners* implies a level of cooperation and trust that sets benchmarking activity apart from other forms of organizational information gathering. For many who are new to benchmarking, the concept of partnering requires some reassessment of their relationships with individuals who are employed in other organizations, especially competitors.

Box 7 (recognized, acknowledged, identified). The process of benchmarking involves an initial investigation to discover the names of companies that are known to be excellent in the area examined. This initial investigation usually involves contacts with experts on the subject being benchmarked: industry experts or analysts, trade or professional associations, and consultants. The investigation also includes printed materials such as professional publications, business press, and popular press. Thus the list of organizations considered for analysis is likely to be more extensive than the list that might be generated based simply on personal experience, acquaintance, or memory. The key concept here involves a preliminary phase of investigation to expand the list of potential benchmark partners.

Box 8 (best-in-class, world-class, representing best practices). The organizations chosen for investigation and analysis represent as close to the state of the art as possible for the subject being benchmarked. Often the identification of these organizations is achieved after considering a larger selection of renowned organizations.

Box 9 (organizational comparison, organizational improvement, etc.). The purpose of benchmarking usually includes some reference to comparisons and change. Once a benchmarking activity is completed, there is a call to action that may involve a variety of activities, from the making of recommendations to the actual implementation of change based (at least partially) on the benchmarking findings. The bottom line in this case is a direction to do something.

Benchmarking as "Learning"

I was once asked to make a benchmarking presentation to an audience of senior scientists at the headquarters of a large pharmaceutical company. The manager in charge of the event was very thorough in briefing me on the audience's credentials and their requirements regarding the presentation. He was also particularly concerned that I find some way to gain the audience's acceptance of and interest in the concept of benchmarking. After all, these types of professionals had built their reputation on basic research and development, and they might not be supportive of a process that focuses attention on the research practices of "outsiders." After thinking about his comments, I proposed that the definition of benchmarking be presented within the context of "learning." Specifically, I wanted to position the concept of benchmarking as another form of professional development that compliments the other kinds of ways that people learn. I began the presentation by asking the audience how they learned and grew as professionals. Their answers included mention of professional journals, professional associations and networks, and personal contacts with other professionals in their fields of specialization. Within this framework, benchmarking made considerable sense and complimented their existing methods of professional development.

This incident always comes to mind whenever someone asks me to give a quick definition of benchmarking. I always include the element of learning and professional development in my response. Perhaps the simplest one-phrase response to the definition question would include some reference to "learning from others." It is important to remember that behind all of the planning and organizing and analyzing activities that define the benchmarking experience lie the fundamental objectives of learning something new and bringing new ideas into an organization. A term that has gained importance in the past few years is *the learning organization.* One of the implications of this concept is that organizations need to step outside of themselves and scrutinize their internal view of the world. This is done when one "exposes" one's own thinking and makes that thinking open to the influence of others. Within this context, benchmarking becomes a fundamental tool that can guide people through the process of looking to the outside for ideas and inspiration—in essence, a tool for the learning organization.

Types of Benchmarking

There are several types of benchmarking activities, and each is defined by the "target" or "object" of the benchmarking activity. As you review the definitions of the different types of benchmarking, remember that the basic process of benchmarking remains the same. Exhibit 1-3 presents a summary of the three major types of benchmarking.

Internal Benchmarking

In many organizations, specific business practices are performed in more than one location, one department, one division, or even one country. Many organizations begin in their benchmarking activities by comparing business practices internally. The company does not assume that it will discover "best business practices" in this effort; it is merely a starting point to begin to identify the best internal business practices in the organization. In other words, the benchmarking learning process begins at home.

Internal benchmarking assumes that there are differences in the work processes of an organization as a result of differences in geography, local organizational history, the nature of managers and employees in different locations, and so on. Internal benchmarking assumes that some of the work processes that exist in one part of the organization may be more effective or efficient than the work processes in other parts of the organization. The objective of the internal benchmarking activity is to identify the internal performance standards of an organization. Often a significant amount of information sharing accompanies internal benchmarking. Many organizations are able to realize immediate gains by identifying their best internal business practices and then transferring that information to other parts of the organization.

Many organizations, such as DEC, AT&T, and Du Pont, advocate

Exhibit 1-3. Types of benchmarking.

Type	Definition	Examples	Advantages	Disadvantages
Internal	Similar activities in different locations, departments, operating units, country, etc.	▪ U.S. manufacturing practices vs. Fuji (Japan) Xerox practices ▪ Marketing strategies by division (copiers vs. workstations)	▪ Data often easy to collect ▪ Good results for diversified, "excellent" companies	▪ Limited focus ▪ Internal bias
Competitive	Direct competitors selling to same customer base	▪ Cannon ▪ Ricoh ▪ Kodak ▪ Sharp	▪ Information relevant to business results ▪ Comparable practices/technologies ▪ History of information gathering	▪ Data-collection difficulties ▪ Ethical issues ▪ Antagonistic attitudes
Functional (generic)	Organizations recognized as having state-of-the-art products/services/processes	▪ Warehousing (L. L. Bean) ▪ Shipment status tracking (Federal Express) ▪ Customer service (American Express)	▪ High potential for discovering innovative practices ▪ Readily transferable technology/practices ▪ Development of professional networks ▪ Access to relevant databases ▪ Stimulating results	▪ Difficulty transferring practices into different environment ▪ Some information not transferable ▪ Time-consuming

and virtually insist that all benchmarking efforts begin with a thorough understanding of their own internal workings before any venture into the outside world. This internal knowledge becomes the baseline for all subsequent investigation and measurement involving external benchmark partners. It also encourages employees to communicate across organizational boundaries—an activity that is not as common as one might think in large or diversified organizations. In fact, internal benchmarking efforts in companies with strong decentralized cultures may be more difficult than benchmarking with outsiders. On a positive note, in many cases, benchmarking has helped bridge the gaps that divide organizations by encouraging internal communications and joint problem solving.

Internal benchmarking is not intended as a substitute for competitive or generic benchmarking activities (which are described in the following sections). In many large and diversified organizations, the internal benchmarking effort alone may involve a lengthy and complex process. Some benchmarkers may feel that because they have collected such a diverse set of information internally, they do not need to add much in the way of external information. This can be a problem if the information collected internally represents a limited focus on the issue being benchmarked or if an organizational bias somehow permeates the findings.

Competitive Benchmarking

Competitive benchmarking involves identification of the products, services, and work processes of your organization's direct competitors. The objective of competitive benchmarking is to identify specific information about your competitors' products, processes, and business results and then make comparisons with those of your own organization.

Competitive benchmarking is useful in *positioning* your organization's products, services, and processes relative to the marketplace. In many cases, the business practices of your competitors do not represent best-in-class performance or best practices. However, this information is valuable because your competitors' practices affect the perceptions of your customers, suppliers, shareholders, potential customers, and "industry watchers"—all of whom have a direct effect on your eventual business success.

There are also other advantages to competitive benchmarking. In most cases, the organizations that are being benchmarked use technologies and business practices that are identical or at least similar to your own. Often your competitors have other things in common with you, such as access to marketing channels, available labor pools, or foreign suppliers. The identification of any similarities becomes a possible advantage when benchmarking. In many cases, the lessons learned from competitors can be applied to your organization without a lot of "translation." For example, a team from General Motors can benchmark the process of painting automobiles with any other car manufacturer in the world and immediately recognize opportunities for assimilation or improvement, because the technologies and processes are so similar (although not identical) among car manufacturers.

Another advantage of benchmarking competitors is that they may have performed their own benchmarking studies and may be willing to trade information. These types of information exchanges are commonplace in many industries, but basic rules relating to sensitive or proprietary information obviously apply.

In some cases, competitors may actually join forces to participate in joint benchmarking projects in nonproprietary areas. These joint efforts may involve investigations outside the industry group, but they usually include the sharing of information among competitors. These types of projects are often initiated or sponsored by an industry group or consortium that attempts to stimulate information sharing for the mutual benefit of its constituent members. An example of this type of group is SEMATECH, a consortium of fourteen American semiconductor manufacturers including companies such as DEC, Hewlett-Packard, Intel, IBM, Motorola, and Texas Instruments. The SEMATECH companies have shared a tremendous amount of information with one another in the area of total quality management practices. Another example of benchmarking coordination among competitors is an effort called the Telecommunications Benchmarking Consortium, made up of approximately eighteen companies, many of which are in direct competition with one another (e.g., AT&T, Bell Atlantic, MCI, Ameritech, GTE). This group established an initial charter that, in part, specifies the desire to benchmark major processes of common interest.

Dancing With the Enemy

One might anticipate all sorts of difficulties when benchmarking among competitors, and the issue must indeed be approached with sensitivity and caution. Interestingly, many organizations admit that one of the greatest barriers to this type of benchmarking is themselves. Traditional stereotypes of competitors as untrustworthy or as the enemy get in the way of basic communication among competitors. A participant in a benchmarking training session that I was conducting became extremely agitated during the portion of the seminar that dealt with competitive benchmarking. Evidently, the mere thought of such an activity violated everything she had ever been taught about dealing with competitors. After much ranting about the evils of collusion, she excused herself from the session and said that she would never "submit to dancing with the enemy." Needless to say, the seminar ground to a screeching halt and we stopped to address this issue in more depth. I asked the seminar participants to write down their thoughts on the subject. I collected unsigned comments and read them to the class. Their fears were typical: "Competitors can't be trusted to give me their 'real' data." "Our attorneys will never allow it." "Why would they [the competitors] want to cooperate with me?" "We want to beat them, not train them!"

In order to respond to this concern, one must accept the fundamental concept that benchmarking is different from doing a traditional competitive analysis. Your benchmark partners should be approached in an up-front manner, with no hidden agendas. Your purpose and your methods are presented to partners for consideration before they are formally asked to participate. You immediately begin to try to establish a benchmarking relationship based on elements of trust and respect. If you approach a competitor as you would an enemy, you will elicit the predictable reaction of suspicion. An honest, professional approach to competitive benchmarking most often produces an honest, professional response from a competitor.

Those who have never participated in a benchmarking project with a competitor will often talk themselves out of using the process before they even get started. Their own fears and antagonistic attitudes are probably more of an obstacle than the attitudes and perceptions of their competitors. I have found that there is virtually no way to convince someone of the attributes of competitive benchmarking by simply talking about it. The possibilities and potential of competitive benchmarking are usually realized as one gains experience with the process.

Functional/Generic Benchmarking

Functional benchmarking involves the identification of products, services, and work processes of organizations that may or may not be your organization's direct competitors. The objective of functional benchmarking is to identify best practices in any type of organization that has established a reputation for excellence in the specific area being benchmarked. The word *functional* is used because benchmarking at this level most often involves specific business activities within a given functional area such as manufacturing, marketing, engineering, or human resources. Perhaps the most frequently cited example of functional benchmarking is the experience of Xerox Corporation and L. L. Bean. After some investigation of warehousing and material-handling operations, L. L. Bean was identified as an industry leader in its order-fulfillment and warehousing operations. Xerox then initiated a benchmarking site visit with the L. L. Bean people and began the process of learning about L. L. Bean's warehousing and ordering processes.

In a functional benchmarking investigation, functional experts from one organization generally limit their benchmarking investigation to their own area of functional expertise. The key distinction in this type of benchmarking is that it can focus on any organization in any industry—the common element being the analysis of excellent business practices.

Another term that is often used to describe this type of benchmarking is *generic*. The word *generic* suggests "without a brand," which is consistent with the idea that this type of benchmarking focuses on excellent work processes rather than on the business practices of a particular organization or industry.

Opportunities for "Breakthrough" Thinking

Organizations with benchmarking experience have provided many examples of the benefits of functional benchmarking outside of their industry groups. The advantages of functional benchmarking can be described in the context of *paradigm shifts*, which often involve radical alterations in an organization's approach to certain issues or problems. One marketing manager from Procter & Gamble complained of inbreeding among companies that compete in the health and beauty aids industry. Although the primary industry competitors had implemented new approaches in the development of the "account team" concept, he stated that many of the new ideas and breakthroughs had been stimulated by examining the marketing structures of computer and office equipment companies. These breakthrough ideas could come only from outside the industry, according to that manager. The long-standing and historically successful patterns that had developed in the industry over the years had bred complacency in the decision-making process—almost an immunity to new ideas.

Functional benchmarking requires the ability to keep an open mind when considering the business practices of a company in another industry group. A benchmarking specialist from Alcoa said it best when he stated:

> You have to think more of what you have in common with these companies and not fall into the trap of trying to critique your differences. Many of our people have a hard time trying not to defend or explain their differences. We often have a harder time just listening and trying to understand than we would like to admit. Perhaps we have been conditioned to believe that we are unique and that we can't learn from anybody else.

The good news is that many companies claim that the ability to maintain an open mind and develop effective listening and observation skills accelerates and improves as people gain experience with the process of benchmarking. However, these companies also advise you to prepare employees who contact external organizations for the possibility of having their assumptions challenged. Again, the good news is that people are better able to prepare themselves psychologically for this type of challenge as they gain experience with the process.

Why Use Benchmarking?

Organizations use benchmarking for a variety of purposes. Some organizations position benchmarking as part of an overall problem-solving process with a clear mandate for organizational improvement. Others position benchmarking more as a proactive mechanism to keep themselves aware of state-of-the-art business practices.

Thinking "Out of the Box"

The most straightforward answer I ever got to the question of why use benchmarking was from an engineer in Illinois who managed a product design center for a farm equipment manufacturing company. We were

Exhibit 1-4. Thinking "out of the box."

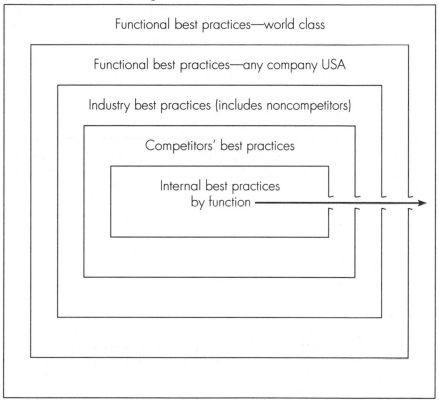

Functional best practices—world class

Functional best practices—any company USA

Industry best practices (includes noncompetitors)

Competitors' best practices

Internal best practices
by function

in one of those restaurants that uses sheets of butcher paper as table-cloths. This particular establishment also provided a jar of large crayons for their more creative diners. As he gave me his answer, he proceeded to draw a series of boxes (Exhibit 1–4). He began by drawing a box and, pointing to the center of it, said, "This is the box that we [his department] are in. It is defined by our management, our personal histories, and our work experiences. We have learned what it takes to be successful in our own box, and we have become very good at managing each other to get what we want. We have each carved out a comfortable space for ourselves, and we could exist quite comfortably by staying snug in our own little spaces." He drew another box that surrounded the first box and continued, "On occasion we take a look outside of our box and see what the competition is up to. If our market share is holding and our sales are OK, then we don't bother looking at the other guy for too long. However, if we are in a downturn and there is some pressure on the bottom line, we look outside the box a little longer and analyze the competition. We make some adjustments and hope for the best. We used to call that competitive analysis." He then drew a third box around the first two and continued. "Now with benchmarking, we not only take a more systematic look at our competitors, but we also take a hard look at other companies in our industry that are not necessarily our competitors. We do this because they do a lot of the same things we do, and many of those companies are a lot like us in terms of the technologies and equipment they use, the people they hire, the customers they serve, and the suppliers they do business with. We're sticking our neck further out of the box, and we seem to be able to learn something new each time we look." He drew a fourth box and wrote the words *any company USA*. He said, "Last year we benchmarked a company that made helicopters! We didn't know anything about helicopters a year ago, and to tell you the truth, I still don't know anything about helicopters and, quite frankly, I don't *want* to know anything about helicopters [or, as he pronounced it, "heel-o-copters."] After we did some investigation, though, we concluded that this helicopter company probably did as good a job as we had ever seen at managing the process of handling engineering change notices. Quite frankly, we were terrible at managing the process of change notices. Our cycle time was horrendous and the amount of rework was killing us. We investigated the subject of design changes and identified about ten companies that had a reputation for minimizing design changes and had greatly reduced their cycle times. The helicopter company proved to be the best of the bunch. We virtually redesigned our entire process using its model, and the turnaround in my department has been incredible." I thought he had drawn his last box when he drew another one and wrote *World-Class*. He leaned over and almost in a whisper said, "And the darndest thing was that the people at the helicopter company told us that they had patterned their process after a German company." He leaned back in his chair and smiled and said, "Do you know what benchmarking has taught us? It taught us that we don't have all the answers, and if we're going to find the answers to our problems, they sure ain't gonna pop up in our backyard!" He pounded his finger back in the middle of the first box and said, "If this business is going to survive in the long

Exhibit 1-5. Why benchmarking?

• Strategic planning	Developing short- and long-term plans
• Forecasting	Predicting trends in relevant business areas
• New ideas	Functional learning; thinking "out of the box"
• Product/process comparisons	Comparing competitors or best-practices organizations
• Goal setting	Establishing performance goals in relation to state-of-the-art practices

run, we better get used to the idea of looking outside of our safe little box—doing it often and doing it right."

The "box" story is important because it's a bottom-line example of the kind of attitude and message that benchmarking encourages. The company in Illinois that employed the engineer in the story did not use the analogy or the words *thinking out of the box*, but in a real way that's the message that reached a lot of its employees. In fact, the formal message of that company had to do with the idea of learning and bringing ideas into the business. The key is that the company created an impression in the minds of its employees that benchmarking was an active process of discovery and that it was a desired activity. It also provided the proper instruction and support that signified a commitment to the process.

One point is clear: Organizations that begin the benchmarking process with a clear purpose or objective have greater success than those that undertake a benchmarking effort without a sense of purpose or direction. Companies that have strongly integrated benchmarking into their cultures have spent a good deal of effort defining and positioning benchmarking in the minds of their employees. They have, in a sense, provided an adequate rationale for the use of the process by creating an awareness of the process and its benefits as well as an expectation that the process should be used in certain situations.

Exhibit 1-5 lists some of the reasons organizations use the benchmarking process. They are not listed in any particular order.

Strategic Planning

Strategic planning requires a thorough knowledge of the marketplace, the likely activities of the competition, the state of the art regarding products or services being produced, financial requirements for doing business in a market, and the customer base (the list could go on). Benchmarking is a useful tool for gathering information in these areas during the process of strategic planning. This type of information can literally shape a business strategy in a more realistic direction, or at least help identify the risks of doing business in certain markets.

Forecasting

Benchmarking information is often used to gauge the state of the marketplace and to forecast market potentials. Benchmarking also provides a source of information regarding the business directions of key players in the marketplace, trends in product/service development, patterns of consumer behavior, and so on.

In many industries, the business direction of a few major companies can shape the direction of an entire marketplace (e.g., IBM, McDonald's, Exxon, American Airlines). Forecasting the activities of these types of organizations often provides their competitors and support-services companies with important information about future implications for their businesses. Industry analysts often gauge the direction of entire markets based on the business activities of just a few companies. This same approach is now used by companies as an integral part of their forecasting activities.   •

New Ideas

Benchmarking is an excellent source of business ideas. One of the primary benefits of large-scale benchmarking is that it exposes individuals to new products, work processes, and ways of managing company resources.

By definition, benchmarking requires that individuals establish formal contacts outside their organizations. In many cases, the process of benchmarking involves personal visits outside the organizational facilities. This is a rare experience for many organizations and for many employees who participate in the process. The reward is exposure to different ideas and approaches to conducting business. IBM originally considered the benchmarking process as an effective means of identifying and closing gaps between its performance and what it considered to be best practices. The same thinking shaped the development of benchmarking at Xerox. Over the years, however, both companies have recognized the benefits of benchmarking purely as a learning experience and its potential as a tool to stimulate the transfer of new ideas into their businesses. Although closing gaps is still an important driver of benchmarking activities in these companies, the stimulation of new ideas and the exposure to new ways of doing business have become sufficient reasons for initiating the benchmarking process.

Not all of the ideas or business practices that are uncovered during benchmarking are going to be useful to an organization. In fact, in many cases the ideas may have little practical utility. However, benchmarking causes people to think about potential ways of conducting business. Benchmarking also provides an opportunity for employees to think "out of the box"—to consider alternative paradigms and to engage in "what if" thinking.

Product/Process Comparisons

A common type of benchmarking activity involves the collection of information about the products or processes of competitors or excellent companies. This information is often collected and used as a standard of comparison for similar products or services of the benchmarking organization. This type of benchmarking conforms most closely with traditional competitive intelligence activities. In these situations, a competitor's product or service is compared feature by feature with the product or service of the company performing the analysis.

This type of benchmarking can also take on a generic flavor. A product or service produced by a noncompetitor (including producers from other industries) may be analyzed to gain insight into factors such as design, product quality, service support, or production processes. The business products or processes of excellent companies are often analyzed by noncompetitors attempting to incorporate elements of the business practices of these companies into their own work environments.

Goal Setting

Benchmarking is used as a means of identifying best practices. Although many organizations do not realistically aim to achieve best-in-class levels of results, they do use this information to establish specific product or process objectives. The standards set by excellent companies in many cases define what is possible on a state-of-the-art performance scale. These goals can help organizations accelerate their performance curves as they strive for continual improvement. For example, many small to medium-size companies cannot hope to achieve the levels of performance of excellent companies that have far greater access to technologies, capital, or other resources. However, these companies can benefit considerably by benchmarking specific work processes that are not dependent on organizational resources. Organizations that are entering new markets also find that benchmarking the best practices of established organizations helps them establish goals that accelerate their learning curves and improve their performance.

Organizations have also encouraged their suppliers to use benchmarking practices in order to help them meet quality or production goals. Motorola, for example, has been very active in encouraging its supplier networks to benchmark Motorola and other suppliers as a means of helping the suppliers meet strict quality objectives. By bringing their suppliers into the benchmarking loop, Motorola is able to model many specific activities and behaviors that will become measurable goals for their suppliers.

What to Benchmark?

Just about anything that can be observed or measured can be benchmarked. In the past, the practice of organizational comparisons was somewhat limited to structural or product-related areas—things that could be readily observed. However, experience with benchmarking has greatly expanded the potential areas for investigation. People are often surprised at the quantity and quality of information that is available to those who make a serious effort to find it.

The categories of information that are presented here do not represent an exhaustive list of areas that can be benchmarked. They do represent the most sought-after information that organizations have attempted to gather as part of their benchmarking investigations (see Exhibit 1-6).

Products and Services

Finished products and services that are offered in the marketplace to external customers are a common subject for benchmarking. Often these

Exhibit 1-6. What to benchmark?

• Products and services	Finished goods; product and service features
• Work processes	How a product or service is produced or supported
• Support functions	Indirect labor—not directly associated with the process of production or support, e.g., finance, human resources
• Organizational performance	Costs, revenues, production indicators, quality indicators
• Strategy	Short- or long-term plans; the planning process

finished goods are observed in their retail state and not in the process of production. These products and services are readily available for analysis, although some products and services (e.g., aircraft, supercomputers, classified weapons systems) are not easily procured for analysis.

Often product or service features are the subject of benchmarking instead of, or in addition to, the entire product or service. These features often account for product differentiation in the marketplace. They may be embedded in the product or service itself (e.g., antilock brakes, software features) or they may be features that accompany the product or service (e.g., product financing packages, warranties, free or nominally priced product upgrades).

Product and service benchmarking is often the subject of competitive analysis. Thus, when considering this type of benchmarking, many people question the differences between benchmarking and traditional competitive analysis techniques. In this case, the two activities have a lot in common, particularly when the focus is on one's competitors.

Work Processes

If products and services define the *what* of benchmarking, work processes define the *how*—that is, how the products or services are produced and/or supported. Work processes are often benchmarked in an effort to establish an understanding of design processes, R&D practices, production processes, workplace design, equipment used for manufacturing and testing, work methods, the application of specific technologies, distribution, and so on.

The benchmarking of work processes is often the subject of investigation when examining organizations outside your competitive area. Once an organization has established a reputation for producing world-class-quality goods or services, a lot of interest is generated regarding how this reputation was earned. Much of this interest comes from organizations that engage in totally different kinds of businesses. The belief that drives this interest is that excellent work processes will produce excellent products and services in practically any industry to which they are applied.

Support Functions

Support functions most often involve benchmarking processes and procedures that are not directly involved with the actual production of products or services offered to external customers. These functions often include the activities of departments such as finance, human resources, marketing, and service. The areas of investigation in this case usually involve the activities that support employees and internal customers.

An example of this type of benchmarking is the analysis of employee compensation systems; this might include levels of pay, variety of compensation choices, the process of adjusting compensation levels, and so on. Although this type of benchmarking is virtually identical to the product/service and process benchmarking described earlier, some organizations make a distinction between the investigation of products or processes that affect internal customers (e.g., employee compensation) and those that have a more direct effect on external customers.

Organizational Performance

Organizational performance includes those outcomes that define an organization's bottom-line success—costs (expenses) and revenues (income). In addition, specific performance indicators relevant to the process of production may be the subject of benchmarking investigations (e.g., yields, asset turnover, depreciation rates, cost of capital).

Often, organizations begin the process of asking the "how" question of benchmarking after reviewing information regarding performance data. The performance data of competitors or excellent companies may be stimulating enough to encourage a more thorough analysis of products/services, the processes employed to produce those outputs, and the support systems required to maintain excellent levels of product and service quality.

Strategy

Some organizations benchmark organizational or functional strategies in order to understand how certain companies gain competitive advantage. In the past, the idea of understanding the strategies of one's competitors was fairly commonplace. It was an attempt to analyze the activities of competitors in a broad context and then determine their future activities based on this understanding.

Today, the idea of benchmarking strategies extends well beyond the analysis of competitors and focuses on strategies of almost any organization that has established a reputation for excellence. The focus of strategic benchmarking today is often on a particular functional area and not on overall corporate or industry strategy. For example, an organization that is interested in improving its customer-service strategy might benchmark organizations that have established a strong reputation for effective and/or efficient customer-service strategies (e.g., Nordstrom, Marriott, American Express). Other functions that are commonly benchmarked in the strategy area include distribution, manufacturing operations, marketing, human resources, and finance. In these investigations, the emphasis is not on particular programs, business practices, or work processes, but rather on the broader business principles and assumptions that stimulate the creation and maintenance of those programs, practices, and processes.

In addition to strategies themselves, the strategic planning process is often the subject of benchmarking activity. This subject not only involves the process of establishing a basic plan, but also considers how organizations react strategically to changes such as the introduction of new technologies, competitive actions, and market opportunities.

Benchmarking—What It Is and What It Isn't

Benchmarking, as described in this chapter, is a straightforward concept. None of the principles or techniques of benchmarking introduce any radical or unique concept to what is essentially a structured process of investigation. No organization to date has patented or copyrighted its version of the process, and the accumulated literature on the subject probably accounts for less than two thousand pages. So, given that the process is relatively easy to grasp—and given the fact that almost anyone in any organization can use benchmarking without any extensive formal training—the question is, why do so many people and organizations have problems applying the process? Why do so many benchmarking projects end in failure or disappointment? Virtually every expert, consultant, trainer, and author who has written a descriptive article on the subject of benchmarking has spent time defining and positioning benchmarking and has dedicated a reasonable amount of attention to describing what benchmarking is *not*. However, even in organizations that have established reputations as leaders in the process of benchmarking, there are problems with the process caused by misconceptions about the very nature of benchmarking, what it takes to do it well, the nature of benchmark partnerships, and the application of benchmarking information.

I asked benchmarking specialists in over twenty companies to describe the misconceptions about benchmarking that still exist in their organizations, even though each organization has had considerable experience with the process. I asked them to avoid the theoretical and to cite specific problems with benchmarking that they could attribute to basic misconceptions about the process. Interestingly, this was an easy question for these specialists to answer. Also interesting was the amount of convergence on a very limited set of misconceptions about the nature of benchmarking. Those misconceptions are described here using some frequently described scenarios. A brief rejoinder (what benchmarking *is*) follows each example (see Exhibit 1-7).

Benchmarking is a one-time event. A group of people receives orientation or training on the subject of benchmarking. They are encouraged to engage in a benchmarking investigation. They perform a benchmarking analysis—often successfully—then write a report, congratulate themselves, close the book, and never attempt to use the process again. For these people, benchmarking is a project or a new tool to experiment with or a diversion from the ordinary work routine. For some, the experience may even be stimulating or fun. But somehow the connection between benchmarking and their day-to-day jobs has not been established. Benchmarking has not been successfully integrated into the way

Exhibit 1-7. Benchmarking: what it is and what it isn't.

Benchmarking Is	Benchmarking Isn't
• A continuous process	• A one-time event
• A process of investigation that provides valuable information	• A process of investigation that provides simple answers
• A process of learning from others; a pragmatic search for ideas	• Copying, imitating
• A time-consuming, labor-intensive process requiring discipline	• Quick and easy
• A viable tool that provides useful information for improving virtually any business activity	• A buzzword, a fad

they think about their work or the way they solve problems or learn. In short, benchmarking, for these people, was an event. And you don't have to look too closely at the organizational environment to understand why this might be the case. Often the subject of benchmarking is launched with a great deal of fanfare in an organization, followed by some encouraging words from a senior manager about benchmarking as a way of doing business. Next is a training program that gets everyone ready to perform. Then, after all that, the benchmarkers are off on their own. It turns out that process facilitation support is scarce. There are insufficient funds in the budget to enable the benchmarkers to visit other companies. Their recommendations are met with indifference or their suggestions plunge into a black hole. There is no reward or recognition for the work they have done. None of their normal work load has been allowed to slip. Their peers don't understand what they are doing and suspect that the process is a boondoggle.

Do you think that the group described above will want to participate in another benchmarking project in the future? Do you think this scenario is unusual? The answer to both questions is, unfortunately, no. Yet this is a scenario that occurs even in established benchmarking companies.

When organizations use the word *continuous* to describe the benchmarking process, they do so based on the belief that business practices, methods, and tools are dynamic in nature—they are bound to change over time. Once one accepts the notion of continuous improvement, it becomes easier to accept the premise that functional best practices are moving targets. Information half-life for many organizational activities can be measured in months, not years. Given that this is the case, the process of investigating these best practices must be an ongoing event for companies just to stay *aware* of the state of the art, much less incorporate state-of-the-art practices.

Now, suppose that your employees understand and accept the assumption of benchmarking as a continuous process. How long do you think they will continue to engage in benchmarking activities if the organization does not adequately support and reward benchmarking activities? Even the most ardent believer in any process will get discouraged if adequate support and reinforcement are missing from the environment. A basic lesson from the trenches is that a continuous process needs continuous support.

Benchmarking provides solutions. A benchmarking team analyzes the business practices or results of a company that has been identified as best-in-class. These business practices or results become the solutions to the team's business issues. Team members do not attempt to integrate the information they have collected from their benchmark partner with other information or consider the business environment that influences the benchmark partner's business practices or results. Since the benchmark partner represents best-in-class in their minds, the decision is made to simply adopt the same business practices or assume that its numbers (e.g., production levels, costs, profits, ratios) are the right numbers for them as well.

This scenario often proves to be disastrous. Blindly substituting another organization's business practices in place of one's own is not the intent of benchmarking. Benchmarking is a process of investigating best practices. The information gained from this investigation needs to be incorporated with other information about one's organization as value-added input to the decision-making process.

Benchmarking is copying or imitating. A common reaction to benchmarking from people who don't understand the process or intent—or who don't want to know about it—is that benchmarking is nothing more than copying or imitating. This type of reaction is classified as defensive by benchmarking specialists. People who are not interested in participating in a benchmarking process will find reasons to criticize it without having experienced it. The copying/imitating defense is often used by employees who are resisting the process.

In some situations, however, the explanation of how benchmarking information was applied in an organization may lead people to believe that benchmarking is simply blatant imitation or copying. This may simply be due to inadequate or misleading communications regarding the process. In the worst case, the organization *has* used benchmarking to imitate or copy the activities of another organization.

When asked to produce a word that accurately describes how benchmarking information is used in an organization, many experienced benchmarkers use the word *assimilate*—to learn and understand, to absorb into the system. Another term that is used is *pragmatic*—concerned with practical consequence. These terms more accurately reflect the intent of benchmarking—learning from others and applying that knowledge to one's own business practices in a practical manner.

Benchmarking is quick and easy. On the surface, benchmarking may appear to be a relatively easy process, and in many cases it is. However, someone may attempt to conduct an investigation into a complex issue with a large group of employees without providing adequate process awareness training, group coordination, rationale, or resource support (e.g., time and money). The Nike athletic-wear company has gotten a tremendous amount of mileage out of its ad campaign that emphasizes the philosophy of "just do it." That philosophy may be effective in stimulating people to exercise, but it is not the kind of message that one gives to a benchmarking team embarking on a benchmarking investigation (especially for the first time). In all too many situations, the "just do it" level of direction results in a benchmarking effort that is poor in its execution and disappointing in its results. An AT&T benchmarking specialist said that there is always one person in a group who—after listening to a basic benchmarking orientation presentation—leaves the room thinking, "Hey, this is no big deal; we identify a problem area, write down a few questions, make a few phone calls, pick up on some ideas, work them into the system, and bingo—we've done benchmarking." This specialist said that when she sees these same people a few months later, they tell her how benchmarking really didn't do much for their group or department.

Benchmarking is not difficult. However, it does require a sufficient amount of project planning, process instruction, quality time, staff support, and funding. Of all these requirements, quality time is the most crucial. A question frequently asked by people who are just learning about benchmarking is, How much time does it take—in terms of both individual employee time and overall project length? I polled twenty benchmarking companies on this question and received a fairly consistent reply. First, however, is the requisite qualifier. They all stated that the answer to this question is determined by several factors such as the scope of the project, the level of criticality of the subject being benchmarked, the experience levels of the people doing the benchmarking, and the level of support available to help with the benchmarking effort. However, when pressed for an answer, they made the following generalizations. Individually, plan for a *minimum* of 10 percent of people's time (on a weekly basis), assuming that you are dealing with a benchmarking team of at least three or four people. This percentage could reach as high as 25 percent for high-priority projects or during certain periods in the benchmarking cycle (as in the case of conducting site visits at a benchmark partner's location). In terms of the typical size of a benchmarking team, the average size was four to six. In terms of project length, four to six months was a common range. Again, these are generalizations and represent averages.

The key message is that benchmarking can be a labor-intensive effort. Multiply the number of people on a benchmarking team by the average number of hours per week per person spent benchmarking times the overall length of the project, and you begin to get an idea of the amount of investment that is required. Benchmarking specialists claim that there is significantly less stress to the systems of both individuals and organizations if the amount of time required for benchmarking is overestimated rather than underestimated. Insufficient planning for the amount of time required to conduct a quality benchmarking investigation often results in taking process shortcuts or putting undue stress on the members of the benchmarking team (and, in many cases, your benchmark partners). On a positive note, it was reported that as employees gain experience with the process, they become much more effective at predicting the approximate amount of time and resources required to conduct a proper benchmarking investigation.

Benchmarking is a fad. Unfortunately, benchmarking seems to have a lot of fad potential and will be destined for a "fade" in many organizations. Why? Perhaps because benchmarking is such an easy concept to understand and seems (to a lot of people) to be easy to implement and manage. Because of this perception, benchmarking will not receive the level of attention, training, support, and funding that it really needs to succeed. This lack of proper attention will result in lackluster benchmarking results in many organizations and eventual fade-out.

Consider companies such as Xerox, Motorola, IBM, and Milliken—companies that have been using the benchmarking process for three, five, or even eight years. Why hasn't benchmarking faded in these organizations? There are several good reasons. First, benchmarking is not passively supported or recommended in these companies. It is strongly encouraged and has achieved the status of an expected organizational activity. It is not only *endorsed* by management, it is *practiced* by management. Second, benchmarking has been successfully incorporated into the quality toolbox of these organizations. The process has been successfully integrated with other quality processes and tools such as formal problem solving. For these types of organizations that have established a strong quality culture, benchmarking is positioned as a process that complements established quality practices; it does not compete with them. Third, these companies have provided adequate levels of support for their employees, as evidenced by the quality of training, the amount of process facilitation support, the efforts made to catalog and communicate benchmarking results, and the intent to recognize employees who participate in benchmarking activities. Finally, these companies actively use benchmarking information and incorporate it into their decision-making processes. Benchmarking information is collected for use in making business decisions. Benchmarking information does not sit on a shelf as a benchmarking study; benchmarking information is used to take action.

2

The Benchmarking Process

Benchmarking can be described as a *structured process*. The structure of the benchmarking process is often provided by the development of a step-by-step process model. The images that come to mind when thinking about structured processes or the models they engender are sequences of boxes and arrows—usually too many to remember. However, a structured process should not add complexity to a simple idea. And the structure shouldn't get in the way of the process; for example, leaving step eleven out of a fourteen-step process does not automatically cause the process to fail. Finally, a process model does not have to be unique, considering that formal benchmarking models have been in existence for ten years.

Why a Process Model?

Process models have two basic attributes that make them useful when used appropriately: They provide structure and they provide a common language.

Structure

Before you build a house, you should have a pretty good idea of how it will look after it is built. You know how the house should function upon completion, and you frame it according to that projected use. Once the basic frame of a house is completed, there are many ways that the house can be finished in order to reflect the preferences, tastes, and uses of individual owners. Although the frames for two houses may have a lot in common in terms of appearance and function, the finished products, in this case houses, can vary tremendously. As long as the requirements of the homeowner are satisfied, it doesn't really matter exactly how a house is finished.

Like the frame of a house, a process model provides the basic framework for action. Within that framework all types of variations are possible, and the process can be tailored to fit the specific requirements of the individuals, groups, and organizations that use it. Any type of benchmarking process model should provide an adequate framework for the successful planning and execution of a benchmarking investigation. In addition, it should be flexible enough to encourage people to modify the process to suit their needs and project requirements.

A Common Language

Ideally, models provide maps of action and behavior that can be understood by anyone in an organization. These maps specify logical sequences of activity that, when followed, produce the desired result—in this case, a successful benchmarking investigation. As these models become known within an organization and people gain experience with the benchmarking process, they serve several functions. The model can help interpret any terminology that is required to use the process. For example, the word *recycling* is used at the end of several benchmarking process models to denote the concept of continuous improvement and to encourage the linking of benchmarking activities. The word *recycling*, in a general sense, may stimulate a variety of images in different people's minds. However, putting the word in the context of a benchmarking model helps people interpret the intended meaning of the word.

The various process steps or stages of a model also help to establish a common language among users. Process steps help define clusters of related activities or tasks. For example, the IBM benchmarking model consists of five phases consisting of a total of fourteen steps. Similarly, DEC has a four-phase model that also consists of fourteen steps. Once IBM and DEC employees understand the models, they are able to communicate with their fellow employees about the benchmarking process using a type of shorthand. For example, if an IBM employee from the corporate office in New York is talking to another IBMer in a division in Minnesota and states that she is in phase two of the benchmarking process, the Minnesota employee knows exactly what kinds of activities have already taken place, what types of activities are currently under way, and what specific activities still need to be done. The benchmarking model has provided a special language that enables these employees to communicate effectively about a process that may be relatively new to them.

A manufacturing manager from Xerox related a story about a cross-functional benchmarking team he was asked to join in the middle of a project. Not only were different functional specialists involved (i.e., marketing, engineering, and manufacturing), but the group was multi-divisional and multinational as well. Because Xerox uses a common benchmarking process worldwide, he was not at a disadvantage joining the team at midpoint; he was able to become an immediate participant in the benchmarking process without the need for extensive process briefing. He also noted that group members, who met for two full days per month, were able to get to work immediately at their meetings. The process "map" had created a common set of expectations of what was to be done at each step of the process, and they did not have to spend time discussing what process they were going to use or engage in debates regarding their next steps. To keep them on track, each member of the benchmarking team had a copy of the Xerox ten-step benchmarking process in the plastic sleeve of the three-ring binders they used to record their activities and critical data.

Development of a Generic Benchmarking Process

The idea of developing a generic benchmarking process was something I first considered in 1990, after having attended a presentation on the subject at a regional meeting of the American Society for Quality Control (ASQC). The presenter was from a large company that had implemented a nine-step benchmarking process. As part of his presentation, the speaker showed a slide that summarized the state-of-the-art benchmarking processes his company had studied before it designed and implemented its own process. He talked about the Xerox ten-step process, the Alcoa six-step process, the Florida Power & Light seven-step process, the AT&T nine-step process, and so on. The person sitting in front of me turned to her neighbor and said—fairly loudly—"Uh-oh, model wars." Among the people seated around me who heard this comment there was an immediate sense of recognition about what she meant— that benchmarking was doomed to be a fad. They interpreted the variety of models as a sign that the process was not yet well documented or understood. The term *model wars* has stuck with me ever since.

A few people had attempted to isolate the common generic elements that typified the benchmarking processes that existed at the time. Unfortunately, even these generic process models varied in the number of phases or steps they contained. Also, although these generic models summarized the types of activities that occurred at each phase, they often did not give the readers (or listeners) a hands-on process that they could take back to their own organizations and implement. I decided to develop a generic model that would serve as a framework for action for people who wanted to implement benchmarking in their own organizations. However, I wanted to develop this model not only from my own perspective but from the perspective of companies experienced in the process of benchmarking. I didn't want to propose a model that would be touted as *the* benchmarking model. And I certainly didn't want to enter into any model wars by critiquing other processes. Quite simply, I wanted to summarize lessons learned from the premier benchmarking companies and use this information to develop a model that could provide a new benchmarker with a basic process map and a set of benchmarking do's and don'ts.

Locating Benchmarking Role Models

I began my own search for best-practices benchmarking companies in May of 1991. The criteria that I established for identifying best-practices benchmarkers included the following:

1. The organization had to use some type of organized process for benchmarking.
2. The benchmarking process had to be incorporated into its normal decision-making process.
3. The process had to be fairly widespread throughout the organization. I didn't want to focus on processes that were understood and applied by only a few people in an organization.
4. The organization had to have demonstrated successful use of the process (meaning that the organization had satisfied its information requirements by using the process and that the people who had used the process felt satisfied with the process and their results).

5. The organization had to be willing to share the results of its process efforts with others.

I began by identifying the possible sources of information I could use to develop a list of premier benchmarking companies. I conducted literature searches on the subject; I called well-established benchmarking companies (e.g., Xerox, Milliken); I talked to quality consultants. From this preliminary search, fifty-seven companies were identified as potential subjects for further investigation. I then constructed a set of eighteen question areas that would be used as the basis for interviewing these companies. These question areas covered subjects such as their use of a structured process, benchmarking training, applications of benchmarking information, resources committed to support the process, project management issues, commonly used sources of benchmarking information, data-gathering and analysis techniques, and legal and ethical issues.

After conducting these preliminary interviews, I reduced my list to twenty-four companies for more in-depth analysis (the names of these companies are listed in the Acknowledgments). What happened to the other thirty-three companies? For one reason or another they did not meet the criteria that had been established. Many of these companies had a relatively small number of employees who had conducted benchmarking investigations, and their processes had not been officially adopted. In fact, not many people in these companies even knew that benchmarking investigations had taken place. Other companies were classified as subscribing to the "just do it" school of benchmarking. They were trying to learn about benchmarking while simultaneously conducting benchmarking investigations. Another group of companies had just started the process of benchmarking and had not yet completed a single benchmarking project. Although their intentions were good, they had not yet put many of their plans into action.

Requirements for a Successful Benchmarking Model

I followed up with another round of interviews with the twenty-four remaining companies. Most of the people I interviewed included benchmarking as one of their major organizational responsibilities or as their sole responsibility. About half of these people had the word *benchmarking* in their job titles. I also interviewed at least two benchmarking experts in each of the twenty-four companies. I expanded the original question list and included additional inquiries about the requirements for a successful benchmarking process. In particular, I asked, "If you were to design a generic benchmarking process model, what features would that model have?" I was looking for some level of consensus regarding the general requirements from this experienced group of benchmarkers.

Many specific recommendations were made by these benchmarking experts. However, four general guidelines also emerged during the course of the interviews.

1. *Follow a simple, logical sequence of activity.* Keep the process model as basic as possible. Do not add process steps for the sake of "numerical superiority." Fourteen steps are not necessarily better than six steps. Although each of these organizations had process models with varying numbers of steps or phases, a basic analysis of their models produced a not-too-surprising result. For the most part, the actual behaviors and actions proposed by these models were virtually interchangeable.

Most of these models were fairly logical in their sequence, but some models included steps that were not specifically related to benchmarking; they seemed to be included more as exhortations to perform some activity that might support the benchmarking effort. For example, the benchmarking process at AT&T's Materials Management Division had twelve steps (three more steps than the corporate nine-step process). Step two of this process model was stated as "Advance the clients from the literacy stage to the champion stage." Although this step was added to encourage communication and increase employee awareness of the process, it did not alter the basic corporate benchmarking model. Other benchmarking process models also contained similar recommendations, but these recommendations did not take the form of actual process steps in the models themselves. The terminology used in the various models was very similar. One simply has to accept the fact that one organization's step is another organization's phase is another organization's sub-bullet, and so on.

The basic message here is not about the terms *steps* or *phases* or the numbers of steps or phases, but about clarity. Perhaps the best measure of a process model's level of clarity is people's ability to describe it to others, including their ability to explain why each part of the process is important to the process user. Another aspect of the clarity criterion is the listener's ability to understand the process and translate it into action.

2. *Put a heavy emphasis on planning and organization.* The second requirement is a heavy emphasis on the planning and organizing activities that occur before any actual contact is made with a benchmark partner. The types of activities included in this part of the process involve developing a clear understanding of the benchmarking "customer" requirements (*customer* referring to the eventual user of the benchmarking information), procuring adequate resources (e.g., people, time, funding) to enable the benchmarking team to fulfill its mission, selecting and briefing members of benchmarking teams, using effective project planning tools and techniques, developing specific information-gathering tools prior to actual data collection, and establishing appropriate benchmarking protocols that define expected behavior toward benchmark partners.

Benchmarking companies strongly emphasize that these planning and organizing activities are not prerequisites but integral parts of the benchmarking process. They warn that many new benchmarkers are anxious to get to the real meat and potatoes of the process—namely contacting partners and gathering data. However, most benchmarking failures cited were caused not by a lack of cooperation on the part of benchmark partners but by an inadequate level of planning and preparation on the part of the benchmarkers themselves. This emphasis on planning and organizing is apparent in virtually every mature benchmarking process model. For example, in the AT&T Materials Management twelve-step process, the planning and organizing activities occupy the first eight steps of the process. In Alcoa's six-step process, data collection and analysis do not take place until step four. A benchmarking manager at IBM stated that of the fourteen steps in its process model, only seven are unique to the benchmarking activity itself; the others are preparatory steps that focus on the project management aspects of the process. However, he added that these project management steps are essential to the success of the benchmarking activity.

3. *Use customer-focused benchmarking.* Benchmarking is a process that produces information as a product. Successful benchmarking organizations treat the benchmarking information product just as they would any other type of product. The product must meet customer requirements if it is to be accepted and used. In this sense, every benchmarking product has a customer or a set of customers. In some cases the customer is the person or team that actually performs the benchmarking analysis. In other cases it may be a manager who commissions a team

to conduct a benchmarking analysis. There may also be multiple customers for benchmarking information. Each customer, however, has a set of requirements or expectations regarding the benchmarking information needed.

A customer-focused benchmarking process places a heavy emphasis on establishing contact with benchmarking customers and using some type of formal process to identify specific customer requirements regarding the benchmarking process, protocol, and information itself. This contact needs to be established very early in the benchmarking process. One of the key advantages of a customer-focused process is that it provides direction and creates a set of expectations regarding how the information is to be gathered, reported, and used. This direction helps benchmarkers avoid wasting their efforts (and the efforts of their benchmark partners) during the course of their benchmarking investigation. Also, once a set of customer requirements has been established, it can be reviewed, negotiated, or adjusted based on a formally agreed-upon contract. (Customer requirements are discussed in more detail in Chapter 3.)

4. *Make it a generic process.* This means that the benchmarking process should be consistent within an organization. Although there should be some flexibility in any process to accommodate some level of variation (remember the house frame example), there is no need for a unique benchmarking process model for every department, division, or location in an organization. Many organizations complain of internal model wars. When different segments of the organization try to develop their own "improved" versions of the process, they are often unwittingly creating barriers between one another. The result is a movement away from a common organizational benchmarking language. The ability to develop cross-functional or cross-divisional benchmarking teams is hampered by the development of different models.

The problem of multiple models within an organization affects other aspects of benchmarking as well. Different models and approaches to benchmarking usually indicate the existence of different communications and training programs that must be developed and maintained by different segments of the company. The result is an inefficient use of organizational resources, redundancy of effort, and confusion among employees who are confronted with a variety of different models within their own organization. Another problem is confusion among the organization's benchmark partners. When approached by different divisions or functions of the same company, benchmark partners should rightfully expect some level of consistency among the approaches used by the various subgroups. One organization polled its various divisions and found that there were five distinct models of benchmarking being deployed under the organization's banner. Many of the organization's benchmark partners were confused by this lack of process conformity and complained that the lack of coordination among the divisions was forcing them, as information providers, to produce redundant reports.

Another problem is that multiple models of benchmarking usually indicate multiple benchmarking databases. Thus, the process of producing records of benchmarking projects and benchmarking results is fragmented within an organization. For example, the company that had five distinct models of benchmarking could account for six distinct benchmarking databases. This duplication of effort and lack of coordination could represent a signfiicant cost for multiple-model companies.

Companies would do well to consider the development of a common process model for benchmarking before the situation gets out of control. Without specific guidance or direction from either a corporate function or some type of internal consortium, individual employees will take it upon themselves to initiate the process. Although this initiative allows individuals, departments, divisions, or locations to get started with the process, it ultimately results in a lack of coordination and possibly some confusion among employees and benchmark partners. Companies that have lived through this experience (or are living through it) strongly urge organizations that are new to benchmarking to consider the development of a consistent, generic benchmarking process model. In addition, the activities of internal communications on the subject of benchmarking, training and facilitation support, and database management should also be coordinated whenever possible.

The Five-Stage Benchmarking Process Model

The challenge at this stage of the investigation was to construct a generic benchmarking model that could be applied to any benchmarking project by any type of organization. The objective was to consider the common elements of the various benchmarking models that were working out in the real world and to distill the various process phases and steps into a simple model that incorporated the essential elements of the bench-marking process.

In order to identify the common elements of the twenty-four bench-marking process models, I literally recorded each of them on a very large sheet of paper. (Imagine an organization's benchmaking process model drawn as a flowchart moving left to right across the page, with each stage of the process preceded by a number; the process model of a second organization would be drawn directly below the first, and so on, until all twenty-four models had been recorded on one large page.) The numbers of steps or stages in the benchmarking models recorded in this manner ranged from six to fourteen. By analyzing these flowcharts, it became apparent that these steps and stages had a lot in common. For example, in one organization, the first two steps or stages of their benchmarking process model were equivalent to the first step of a more abbreviated model. That is, both models were trying to convey the need to identify the subject of the benchmarking investigation; one model communicated this in one step, the other in two.

As I continued to analyze the benchmarking process models in this manner, I was trying to identify a basic set of process steps or stages that were common across all of the twenty-four process models. I was attempting to identify a set of "core" steps or stages that would capture the essence of each of the process models being considered. This exercise proved to be easier than I had predicted; while the exact language and the number of specific steps varied somewhat, the overall direction and intent of each of the models were very consistent, making comparisons between the models very easy.

What emerged from this exercise were five stages of benchmarking activity, each defining a unique set of activities and ordered in a logical sequence. The elements of a basic model were falling into place. In order to test the validity of these process stages, I contacted the bench-marking specialists from ten of the twenty-four companies whose mod-els served as the foundation for this generic process. I chose these ten companies based on the fact that each of their models was somewhat different with respect to the number of stages or steps included. I asked them two basic questions. First, did the model make sense to them in the context of their existing models? Second, what suggestions would they make, if any, to change the model? The response to question one was unanimous. The model was concise and understandable and seemed to capture the intent of each of their own models. The answer to the second question was equally supportive; only a few minor

Exhibit 2-1. The five-stage benchmarking process.

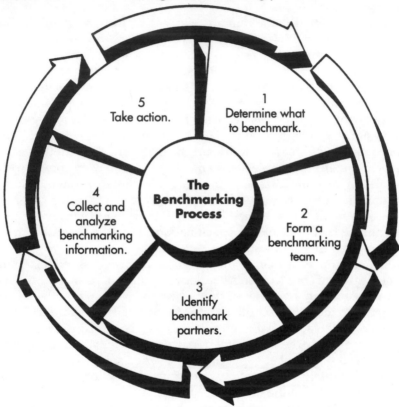

semantic changes were recommended. No additional process steps were added, and none were deleted. The resulting benchmarking model is illustrated in Exhibit 2-1. The five process stages are:

1. *Determine what to benchmark.* This first stage of the process is to identify the customers for the benchmarking information and their requirements and define the specific subjects to be benchmarked. Once the subjects to be benchmarked and the customer requirements are known, the resources required (e.g., time, funds, people) to conduct a successful benchmarking investigation can be identified and secured.

2. *Form a benchmarking team.* Although benchmarking can be con-

ducted by individuals, most benchmarking efforts are team activities. The process of selecting, orienting, and managing a benchmarking team is the second major stage of the benchmarking process. Specific roles and responsibilities are assigned to team members. Project management tools are introduced to ensure that benchmarking assignments are clear to everyone involved and that key project milestones are identified.

3. *Identify benchmark partners.* The third stage of the process involves the identification of information sources that will be used to collect benchmark information. These sources include employees of benchmarked organizations, consultants, analysts, government sources, business and trade literature, industry reports, and computerized databases, to name just a few. Also included in this stage is the process of identifying industry and organizational best practices.

4. *Collect and analyze benchmarking information.* During this stage of the process, specific information-collection methods are selected. It is important that the people responsible for collecting information be proficient in these methods. Benchmark partners are contacted, and information is collected according to an established protocol and then summarized for analysis. Benchmarking information is analyzed in accordance with the original customer requirements, and recommendations for action are produced.

5. *Take action.* This stage of the process is influenced by the original customer requirements and uses for the benchmarking information. The action taken may range from the production of a report or presentation to the production of a set of recommendations to the actual implementation of change based, at least in part, on the information collected in the benchmarking investigation. Any next steps or appropriate follow-up activities are identified, including the continuation of the benchmarking process.

Why a Circular Model?

One of the most entertaining discussions I have ever witnessed took place at Xerox in the late 1980s. A group of managers were debating the shape of a model that was going to be used to describe a new process of adjusting employees' compensation levels. The process consisted of a series of steps that would occur in a certain sequence. The issue was whether the model should be drawn as a flowchart or as a wheel. The discussion had nothing to do with the utility of the shape; it was really just a question of aesthetics (their word, not mine). In the end, they used neither a flowchart nor a wheel—the model ended up being drawn as a time line.

The generic benchmarking model introduced in this book is circular. Is it for reasons of aesthetics? Is there some utility to a circular shape? Does it really make any difference? The answer to all of these questions is yes. One of the surprising things I discovered when conducting my interviews with the benchmarking companies was that every benchmarking process model except one (Alcoa's hexagon) is drawn as a flowchart. The use of a flowchart makes sense, considering that it is a reasonable tool to use to illustrate a sequence of events. However, most of the models include some form of directive in their final step or phase to "recycle" or "recalibrate." The implication is that benchmarking information needs to be reassessed periodically, in recognition of the fact that the products or processes being benchmarked are dynamic and will change over time. The basic message is to continue the benchmarking process as a way of doing business, constantly striving for improvement. However, in my mind flowcharts project a process that has a beginning and an end. The only way to illustrate recycling on a flowchart is to draw a long line connecting the final box with one of the previous boxes in the model.

The message inherent in a model that advocates continuous improvement and recycling brings to mind a circular image. Although the five stages of the benchmarking process do not gain any special meaning by being drawn in a circle, the shape suggests continuity. Note the arrows surrounding the circle. The implication is that the process is active, it is moving, it is continuous. There was also an aesthetic issue that made the circular shape appealing. If you've ever examined the packaging of paper products that utilize recycled materials, you may have noticed that there is a small logo on the packaging consisting of a trio of arrows forming a circle. This logo has become an official national symbol for recycling. It is also used in product advertising and promotional efforts. I felt that the people who designed that logo had captured the essence of recycling. It made aesthetic and practical sense to add the arrows to the circular model to more strongly suggest the concept of recycling the benchmarking process without having to actually say it.

Part Two

The Five Stages of Benchmarking

3

Stage 1: Determining What to Benchmark

The process of determining what to benchmark begins with a fundamental question: Who is the customer for the benchmarking information (see Exhibit 3-1)? *Customer* in this context means *user*. Once the basic requirements of the information users are understood, the process of developing specific measures can begin. Why this focus on the customer? Consider this issue in light of the experiences of companies that have been using the process. One of the most common problems reported concerns the resources needed to conduct a thorough benchmarking investigation. In particular, the amount of time required is often excessive. Another major complaint is that so much of the information collected goes unused. Why are these problems so common among benchmarking companies? Two common explanations are suggested by those same organizations that report the problem.

1. *Haste makes benchmarking waste.* The first is that organizations are anxious to use the benchmarking process. After receiving some basic instruction or direction to benchmark, many organizations charge forward with data collection, cutting a wide path through all sorts of subject areas, tackling broad subjects, and asking open-ended questions. Such an effort produces more questions than answers. In their rush to use this new process, organizations fail in several key areas of benchmarking. They fail to establish a clear mission or purpose for their efforts; they fail to ensure that their own processes are sufficiently understood and documented; they do not thoroughly investigate the

Exhibit 3-1. The benchmarking process: Stage 1.

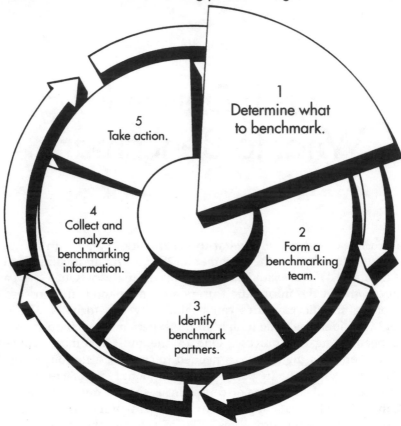

companies that legitimately represent best practices; they do not prepare adequately for their meetings with benchmark partners; and the list could go on. The result is a poorly planned and executed benchmarking effort.

2. *The target is too big.* The largest benchmarking report I ever saw was over 850 pages. It was ten months in the making (and required ten months in the reading as well). The problem with the report was that it covered just about every aspect of the subject—in this case, employee communications practices. The report was developed by a staff of internal communications managers in a medium-size company that

manufactured medical diagnostic equipment. Their process of identifying the subjects of their benchmarking investigation consisted of a brainstorming exercise in which every possible aspect of employee communications was identified. The list included over eighty-five variables, many of them with broad titles such as "newsletters." The managers then brainstormed the names of companies that they considered to be excellent in the area of employee communications. They divided up the companies (over thirty of them) among themselves and began a process of interviewing a communications specialist in each company—attempting to cover all eighty-five variables in each interview. When they produced their final report, their recommendations to management took up two pages. Only a few action items resulting from the report were ever considered for implementation in the company. The leader of the benchmarking team was disappointed because so much of the information collected was too general to be useful, and no one even read the entire report (the executive summary alone was over forty pages). When asked to summarize what the team had learned from this experience, the leader responded, "The target was too big."

The lessons learned by this company are important to remember. First, identify subjects for benchmarking based on some type of critical need. Do not attempt to analyze an entire process or product simply because you can. (This is discussed later in this chapter under the heading "Identifying Critical Success Factors.") Second, create measures that are as specific as possible. When you are discussing issues with benchmark partners, specific measures will more likely put you in common territory with them. For example, instead of starting out with the broad category of "newsletters," the team mentioned earlier should have broken the subject into more specific, measurable areas such as newsletter types, budgets, distribution, production processes, staffing, or document formatting.

Defining the Customers for Benchmarking Information

The first step in developing a benchmarking plan and deciding what to benchmark is the identification of the customer for the benchmarking information—quite simply, who is requesting the information and who will use it? This step is important for the following reasons:

■ *The customer identifies specific information requirements.* The customer is, in most cases, an individual or group with a critical need. Motivated by some factor or combination of factors (e.g., market conditions, new competition, new technologies, performance problems/opportunities), the customer begins the process by identifying the products, services, or processes that need to be benchmarked. The key to these information requirements is *need*. Benchmarking should not be used as a general data-gathering technique to test markets or survey what's going on among other companies or as a means for establishing contacts in other companies.

The customer can also provide specific examples of the types of information to be collected during a benchmarking investigation. For example, the customer can take a fairly broad subject area that has been identified for investigation and improvement, such as billing, and identify specific facets of the billing process that are driving the interest in benchmarking (e.g., billing cycle times, the format of the billing statement itself, the computer software used for billing). Not only can customers identify specific kinds of information, they also can provide examples that illustrate the desired format and level of specificity (e.g., ratios, dollars rounded to the nearest ten thousand, product specifications). This level of specificity ensures that the information gathered from benchmark partners is comparable to the information being analyzed in the customer's organization.

The customer can also identify specific companies or types of companies that should be included in the benchmarking investigation. Although some of these companies may not ultimately meet the criteria used to define best practices, they do provide an indication of the level of contact and general caliber of company desired. This type of pre-investigation identification also provides clues regarding the basic criteria for organizational selection that the customer has in mind.

■ *The customer establishes a time frame for completion of the benchmarking investigation.* The customer can identify not only the expected completion date, but also key delivery dates or interim project checkpoints. These interim expectations may involve the production of progress reports, presentations, or preliminary analyses. The customer also plays a key role if the project delivery dates are required to change. The customer will, in most cases, define the level of flexibility of the project plan.

■ *The customer often provides the necessary funding/support for the benchmarking activity.* Once the subjects of the benchmarking investigation are identified and the time line set, the customer is usually responsible for providing the necessary resources. These resources include the people who will actually perform the benchmarking task, the staff support (e.g., legal, MIS, administrative assistance), and the funding (e.g., travel expense, telephone expense, report preparation expense).

Another way to define benchmarking customers is to ask, who will use the benchmarking information? Or, whose requirements need to be understood before launching a benchmarking investigation? When this question was posed to experienced benchmarkers, their responses indicated that there are several key customer types that should be considered when defining the benchmarking customer base.

The Commissioning Manager

In many organizations, the stimulus to engage in benchmarking is generated by a manager or group of managers who, after determining a need for benchmarking information, commission an individual or a team to conduct a benchmarking investigation. This commissioning may take the form of a task force or task team assignment for a cross-functional or interdivisional group. The more likely situation is for a manager to assign the benchmarking task to an intact work group in the manager's functional area. In some cases, the commissioning manager is part of the benchmarking team, acting as either team leader or a regular member. In many situations, however, the commissioning manager does not participate on the team. The expectation is that the benchmarking team will summarize its findings and produce a report of its investigation and a set of recommendations for the commissioning manager. The locus of action, in this case, is in the commissioning manager and not necessarily in the benchmarking team. In some situations, the commissioning manager also creates an expectation that the benchmarking team will take specific actions on its own as a result of the benchmarking analysis.

Some organizations, such as Xerox and Du Pont, use the word *sponsors* to describe the managers who initiate benchmarking activities. At Xerox, these types of sponsored benchmarking projects are usually involved with strategic benchmarking projects (as opposed to projects initiated by employees for their own tactical purposes). At AT&T, approximately two-thirds of the benchmarking projects are commis-

sioned. However, there is a desire to decrease the number of commissioned projects that result in reports or recommendations and stimulate
more hands-on benchmarking projects by teams that are empowered to
make changes in the work environment. At DEC, there is a definite
preference *not* to advocate commissioned benchmarking projects that
result in a report or set of recommendations. DEC's preference is to
stimulate teams to perform benchmarking analyses after team members
have determined a need to take action toward self-improvement.

The Benchmarking Team as Its Own Customer

In the vast majority of benchmarking situations, individuals and, more
typically, teams of employees engage in a benchmarking project using
their own initiative. In many cases, benchmarking has been positioned
as part of a total quality management toolbox and thus becomes integrated with other quality processes and tools such as structured problem
solving. In these situations, employees are empowered to take action
and initiate benchmarking projects as part of their continuous improvement efforts. In companies that do not have total quality management
systems in place, benchmarking is often positioned as a tool that can be
applied, when appropriate, to any subject in any area of the organization. As long as the initiating individuals or teams can accomplish their
normal work tasks and can gather the necessary resources to conduct a
successful project, they are empowered to initiate a benchmarking
project.

     In most cases, benchmarking teams must receive the approval and/
or support of a manager or sponsor. This is usually part of the normal
approval process that must be exercised whenever a team activity
requires an allocation of work hours or capital. The major objective for
these self-initiating teams is to take action. They decide how to incorporate benchmarking information into their decision-making process
and what action, if any, they will take as a result of their benchmarking
activity. These benchmarking teams generally do not consider the
presentation of findings or recommendations a major objective.

Other Benchmarking Customers

There are at least two other types of customers for benchmarking
information. The first is other employees within the organization who
may benefit from the results of the benchmarking findings. These

employees may be other groups or individuals who perform similar or identical functions in other parts of the company (e.g., other divisions, other departments, other locations). In many cases, they can take full advantage of the benchmarking results produced by a group that performs the identical function. Also, an individual or group that does not perform the identical function may be able to take advantage of the benchmarking information if it deals with a generic issue that is common to both. For example, a benchmarking team at Xerox borrowed heavily from another benchmarking team's report analyzing how to reduce a specific set of overhead costs. The original benchmarking analysis was performed by employees in an engineering department, and the other group was from the manufacturing department. Although their specific functions and, in this case, work locations were different, the recommendations from the original engineering group could be understood and applied by the manufacturing group.

In order to facilitate the sharing of benchmarking information, most large benchmarking organizations have established a database that can be accessed by anyone in the organization. This database can be used to review brief summaries of benchmarking projects categorized by function, date, and location. Other techniques used by organizations to stimulate internal sharing of benchmarking information include special benchmarking newsletters or reports and the development of internal benchmarking consortia (usually functional or divisional in nature).

The second type of potential benchmarking customer includes the actual benchmark partners who participate in the process. Many organizations offer report summaries to their benchmark partners as an inducement and reward for their participation. Some benchmarkers are effective marketers of these benchmarking reports and attempt to anticipate the types of report summaries and report formats that might be attractive to potential benchmark partners.

Determining Customer Requirements for Benchmarking Information

The information needs of benchmarking customers should be explicitly defined before launching a benchmarking activity. The key here is specificity. The immediate benefits of this needs analysis are realized in the planning stages of the benchmarking effort. The customer's requirements affect the benchmarking schedule, the scope of the effort, the format for reporting, and the allocation of resources. Experienced benchmarkers have established the fact that a thorough understanding of the customer's requirements helps avoid the wasted effort of gathering useless information.

Customer Diagnosis

In order to establish the information requirements of your benchmarking customers, you absolutely must spend some quality time with them discussing and documenting their specific benchmarking needs. I refer to this process as a diagnosis, because it resembles the process of a doctor gathering information about a patient before prescribing treatment. There is a medical phrase that says, "Prescription without diagnosis is malpractice." The same can be said about benchmarking. Without adequately assessing the state of your own organization and assessing the needs of your customer, you are prone to commit errors that could cost your organization time and money at the very least, and could possibly cause your organization to make a bad business decision based on inappropriate information.

This process of diagnosis should be the leadoff activity in Stage 1 of the benchmarking process. The format of the diagnosis is to interview those individuals or groups that have been identified as customers for the benchmarking activity. The purpose of these interviews is first to ensure that the individuals engaged in the benchmarking process have a clear understanding of customer requirements. Second, this process often raises important issues that the customer may not have considered, especially if this is the customer's first experience with benchmarking. Often the commissioners of a benchmarking activity do not understand what is involved with the process or what issues need consideration early on. By performing this diagnostic step, you will probably find yourself conducting a minitutorial on the benchmarking process for your benchmarking customer. Third, these interviews formalize the benchmarking requirements of the customer. It is strongly recommended that you document the agreements reached in these discussions. This documentation will serve as a record of the agreed-upon parameters of the benchmarking project. This "contract" protects you from any unanticipated changes in the project requirements as it unfolds. It also serves as a baseline for negotiations for the resources you will need to conduct your investigation.

The following issues should be discussed as part of the preliminary diagnostic process. Although the issues are presented here in a logical sequence, the important point is to cover each of these issues with your benchmarking customer. Even if you and your team are your own customers, you still need to review these issues and feel confident that you understand the nature of your own requirements before you proceed. A summary of the contents of the benchmarking diagnosis is presented in Exhibit 3-2.

Identifying Customers

This includes the identification of specific individuals and groups that will use the benchmarking information. These customers may include the commissioning manager (the sponsor), the actual members of the benchmarking team, and other internal users or potential users of benchmarking information.

An effort should be made to determine how many of the actual customers of benchmarking should be consulted before embarking on the benchmarking investigation. It is worth the time at this stage to anticipate the needs of other parties that may have an interest or a stake in the benchmarking project. These other parties may include other managers or employees whose work, budget, or time may be affected by the outcomes of the benchmarking investigation. It is also recommended that you think proactively in this regard and seek out potential customers for your benchmarking findings. Your efforts to actively solicit inputs at this stage of the process may, in the long run, save you a considerable amount of work or rework. A sign on a benchmarking specialist's desk at IBM summed it up best. It said, "Anticipate the Need."

Types of Benchmarking

The basic emphasis of the benchmarking customer is defined by the desired target of the benchmarking activity. Specifically, is there a need for internal, competitive, or functional/generic benchmarking, or some combination of the three? The intent and direction of the benchmarking customer can be diagnosed by establishing the types of benchmarking desired. For example, a focus on internal and competitive benchmarking indicates an emphasis on competitive positioning. The addition of best practices from a functional standpoint indicates a much

Exhibit 3-2. Customer requirements for benchmarking.

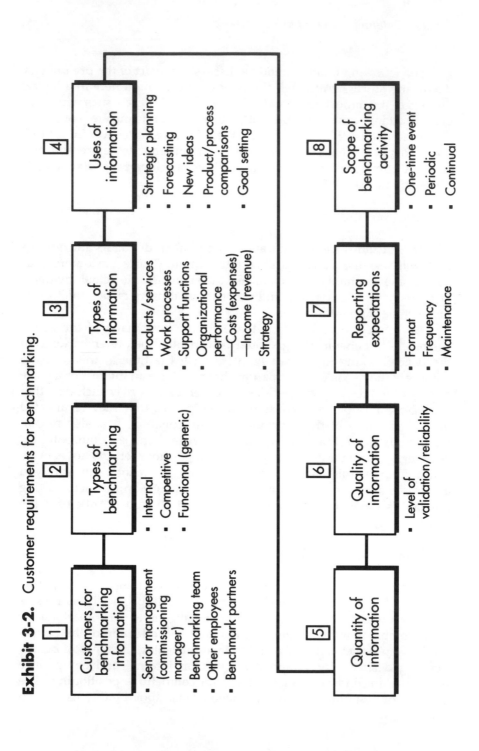

[1] Customers for benchmarking information
- Senior management (commissioning manager)
- Benchmarking team
- Other employees
- Benchmark partners

[2] Types of benchmarking
- Internal
- Competitive
- Functional (generic)

[3] Types of information
- Products/services
- Work processes
- Support functions
- Organizational performance
  —Costs (expenses)
  —Income (revenue)
- Strategy

[4] Uses of information
- Strategic planning
- Forecasting
- New ideas
- Product/process comparisons
- Goal setting

[5] Quantity of information

[6] Quality of information
- Level of validation/reliability

[7] Reporting expectations
- Format
- Frequency
- Maintenance

[8] Scope of benchmarking activity
- One-time event
- Periodic
- Continual

broader charter and implies a more comprehensive examination process.

Types of Information

What is the focus of the benchmarking investigation as defined by the established need? Is the focus on products and services, work processes, organizational performance indicators, or some other aspect of the organization? The implications for benchmarking activities are strongly affected by the breadth of the benchmarking focus. In particular, the magnitude of the benchmarking effort is increased tremendously when benchmarking work processes. Process benchmarking is a complex activity that involves an intense and lengthy effort. If work processes are included as a focus for benchmarking, it is advisable to work with the benchmarking customer to develop a specific process measurement objective. For example, a red flag should appear in your mind when your customer tells you to benchmark the distribution process or benchmark the product-development process. These process directions are too broad and will result in a benchmarking report that takes two people to carry, or else they will produce a general set of findings that do not lend themselves to specific recommendations for action.

Uses of Information

How will the benchmarking information be used? Specifically, is the information needed to make product or process comparisons, to develop strategic plans, as a source of stimulation and new ideas, to set goals? The intended use of the benchmarking information affects the amount of effort required to identify and collect that information. Also, the uses significantly affect your choice of benchmark partners and the types of questions you ask them. If the benchmarking data are to be used for specific product or process comparisons, the level of specificity of benchmarking subjects can be focused and objective. For example, think of a benchmarking project in which the subject of investigation is the electrical components of a driver-side air bag. Contrast this with a project in which the subject of investigation is competitive and best-practices strategies in the area of consumer safety. The relative scope and complexity of these two projects are very different, as are the implications for your time and resources.

Quantity of Information

The amount of information desired is an important aspect of customer requirements. For example, an exhaustive investigation of best-in-class products or best-practices processes could involve hundreds or even thousands of hours of investigation. Limiting a benchmarking activity to a smaller population of potential organizations greatly reduces the quantity of information generated. For example, if a company wanted to perform a benchmarking analysis of the competitive marketing practices in the domestic commercial aircraft industry, the benchmarking activity could realistically be limited to four or five domestic producers that account for 90 percent of the commercial market. If, on the other hand, one wanted to analyze state-of-the-art corporate travel reservation and accounting systems—domestic and international—one might have to engage in a lengthy search of corporate travel accounting practices in a variety of industries and countries in order to discover the true state-of-the-art processes and practices. The quantity of information generated during the investigative stages of this process can be extensive. Therefore, it is important to clarify the expectations of the customer to ensure that it has defined its information requirements realistically and will support the efforts necessary to generate the information requested.

Another aspect of information quantity involves the extent of documentation collected from benchmark partners. For example, a minimal amount of information might include only the information that is recorded during the benchmarking interview. At the other extreme, the benchmark partner may be asked to provide whatever documentation or materials it considers appropriate given the subjects being benchmarked. This could mean hundreds of pages of documentation that will have to be reviewed or cataloged in some way. Multiply this amount of data by the number of organizations included in your investigation, and you could end up with a massive quantity of information. One rule of thumb is never to ask a benchmark partner to send whatever information is appropriate. You may get more than you bargained for.

The level of detail of benchmarking analyses can vary significantly by organization and by project. The level of detail expected by the customer affects the amount of time required to collect, analyze, catalog, and summarize the benchmark information. For example, an analysis of competitive products and services can range from a fairly superficial analysis of product features to a detailed analysis of design processes, production processes, quality control techniques, and so on. The level of detail usually reflects the benchmarker's personal concern with detail, not the amount of information actually available. The amount of detail in benchmarking analyses also varies based on the level of detail that is appropriate for the benchmarking customer. There is a high correlation between the amount of detail included in a benchmarking investigation and the amount of time and resources required to collect and organize that information.

Quality of Information

We assume that all the information collected in a benchmarking investigation is of high quality. However, distinctions such as the level of validation or reliability can be made.

Validation involves the use of multiple sources of information: multiple interviews per location, cross-checking of archival data with the originating source, multiple measures of information over time from the same source. Consider an example: You have identified a particular company as representing best practices in the area you are benchmarking. You have also identified a set of specific measures to review with that benchmark partner. The question is, how many individuals do you interview in that organization before you feel satisfied that your data accurately reflect that organization's products or processes? Are you comfortable attaching the label of IBM or General Motors or Illinois Tool Works to a number that was provided over the telephone by a single individual? Interestingly, most benchmarking companies *do* rely on the report of a single individual to reflect the workings of an entire organization. When questioned about this practice, benchmarkers' rationale was that they had made the effort necessary to identify expert and reliable benchmarking resources. The rest is an act of trust or faith on the part of each individual benchmarker. One thing is certain: Assuring information validity and reliability increases the amount of time and resources required to generate a benchmarking information base.

Reporting Expectations

Customer requirements for the reporting of benchmarking results vary significantly by project, by customer, and by organization. Some benchmarking report formats require extended narratives to describe the benchmarking process and results; some are tabular with very little narrative. The standards for documentation in some organizations can add considerable work to the process of generating a benchmarking report. Some organizations do not generate specific reports at all, but enter benchmarking data into a database in the form of brief project summaries that can be accessed by customers or other employees on an as-needed basis.

In some cases, benchmarking activity is reported in a formal presentation. The preparation of a benchmarking presentation requires additional time and resources and may increase the pressure felt by the benchmarking team.

The frequency of reporting also has implications for those responsible for benchmarking activity. In some cases, reporting is a one-time activity. In others, benchmarking is a periodic or continuous process that requires repeated report generation. The frequency of reporting also affects the resources required for benchmarking.

Information maintenance must also be considered as benchmarking data are collected and organized. Decisions must be made regarding responsibilities for maintaining the benchmarking database (both written documents and on-line databases). For large organizations that make extensive use of benchmarking, some consideration should be given to incorporating benchmarking information with other reports or databases that exist within the organization. Care must also be taken to ensure that the proposed benchmarking activity does not duplicate other benchmarking projects.

The amount of time and resources dedicated to the development, delivery, and maintenance of benchmarking reports varies greatly among benchmarking organizations. There is a definite trend, however, away from the practice of generating extensive reports. Most benchmarking reports attempt to capture the bulk of benchmarking data in a condensed form and focus most of the attention on the summaries and recommendations sections. Unless there is an extensive audience or a critical need for detailed benchmarking analyses, most companies do not advocate the production of lengthy benchmarking reports. However, adequate information archives should be maintained. Most organizations advocate the retention of raw data for a nominal period of time.

Scope of the Benchmarking Activity

The scope of benchmarking refers to the amount of benchmarking activity anticipated over time. The customer requirements on this dimension vary, but they generally fall into one of three categories:

1. *One-time event.* The benchmarking activity is defined as a singular event with a start date and a completion date. It is often a stand-alone project that is not intended to be repeated. These events are often referred to as benchmarking projects rather than processes. In this type of benchmarking, the information requirements are specific and focus on a limited range of information. For example, a large food production company commissions a large-scale benchmarking project during the process of new-product development. The purpose of this project is to position the new product in relation to the top competitive products already available in the marketplace. The company measures consumer reactions to its marketing strategies, pricing, packaging options, and product quality and asks consumers to evaluate those features in relation to competitor's products. The project team also establishes the public perceptions regarding the marketing effectiveness of major competitors and asks consumers to rank companies based on perceived effectiveness of marketing activities. This type of project is not scheduled on a regular basis and may not be employed for every product introduced in a given year.

2. *Periodic activity.* Some organizations conduct benchmarking analyses as a standard business practice and plan their benchmarking activities according to a regular calendar—for instance, annually or quarterly. For example, several large organizations conduct an annual quality audit of their major products and services in relation to those of their competitors or other best-practices companies. The benchmarking effort in this case is usually conducted during the same month or quarter each year.

3. *Continuous activity.* Continuous benchmarking activity is ongoing and is not generally limited to a one-time or periodic event. This type of benchmarking is typical of an organization that has adopted a broad perspective of benchmarking and has incorporated that activity into the goal of continuous improvement of large numbers of managers and employees. For example, Xerox Corporation has trained thousands of employees (including most managers) in benchmarking practices and empowers managers and employees throughout the organization to initiate and conduct their own benchmarking projects. This proliferation of trained and experienced benchmarkers results in a continuous state of benchmarking activity across all departments, locations, and divisions. Xerox has also established benchmarking networks that encourage continuous benchmarking by the sharing of benchmarking data and

the development of cross-functional benchmarking teams. The Xerox benchmarking model also encourages employees to recalibrate their benchmarking information, which implies a continuous effort to benchmark.

A Diagnostic Summary

Once the customer diagnosis is complete, you should record the results of your discussions and produce a diagnostic summary. This summary is simply a review of the issues that were discussed with the benchmark customers and a statement of the agreed-upon parameters that will guide the benchmarking investigation. This summary should be formally documented and routed to all known customers for the benchmarking project, all parties who may have a direct interest in the benchmarking investigation, and all members of the benchmarking team. The time to test for understanding, agreement, and suggestions is early in the process. The diagnostic summary can be an effective tool to elicit useful preproject feedback from all interested parties.

Identifying Critical Success Factors

Perhaps the most important question that can be answered when selecting the subject of a benchmarking investigation is, what factors will have the greatest impact on the performance of the organization? Most companies dedicate a good portion of their benchmarking orientation and training to the issue of criticality. Because benchmarking is often a lengthy and expensive process to support, employees are encouraged to engage in the process only when it appears capable of adding value to the decision-making process. Also, benchmarking is advocated as a valuable tool when decisions may have a significant impact on the bottom-line results of the business. Benchmarking is not the process of choice when investigating routine matters or issues of low to moderate importance. It is also not advocated solely as an information-gathering technique.

Many benchmarking organizations have begun to use a term to refer to subjects that are significant enough to warrant the use of the benchmarking process. The term is *critical success factor*, or CSF. Most benchmarking organizations do not have a formal definition of CSF but use the term to encourage employees to use the benchmarking process selectively on issues of critical import to the organization. Some companies provide examples of appropriate subjects as well as examples of subjects that might be better served by a less costly or complicated process.

In many (if not most) benchmarking studies, the call to action for benchmarking is clear and unambiguous. In some cases, a manager commissions a specific benchmarking project. In others, an individual or team identifies a specific problem or opportunity for benchmarking based on some obvious need. In these situations, the identification of CSFs may be easy and straightforward. However, there are situations in which an individual or team is provided with only a general direction to use the benchmarking process, with no clear indication of the specific subject of the benchmarking effort. It is then the employees' task to generate their own list of CSFs.

The Challenge: Linking CSFs With Meaningful Business Results

The reaction to this benchmarking challenge often results in two dysfunctional choices that are commonly made by novice benchmarkers. The first choice is to select a subject for benchmarking that is easy to define, plan, and execute. The rationale for this choice is to give the team members some exposure to the process by having them focus on a subject that is relatively easy to comprehend and measure. The danger of this choice is that the benchmarking subject borders on the trivial and involves an issue that could be investigated using a much less complex or expensive process. The other danger of this approach is that it creates the impression that the technique works only for trivial subjects.

The second choice that often proves frustrating to novice benchmarkers is the selection of a subject that is so critical to an individual, group, or function that it could be classified as a "make-or-break" issue. The subject selected may be under intense scrutiny by senior management, or it may be a controversial issue that involves a significant level of stress in the organization (e.g., work-force efficiencies and staffing levels). When a new benchmarking team is asked to use this new process to provide critical information on a top-priority issue, the pressure of the situation takes its toll. Team members may focus too much attention on the issue itself and not enough attention on the benchmarking process. The team will also be under intense observation by other employees, including some fairly influential people in the organization. The result is that the team strays from the benchmarking process because of all the distractions related to the issue, or else it panics under the intense pressure. In any event, the process suffers.

Perhaps the best (worst?) example of this was a benchmarking team whose task was to investigate best practices for managing work-force reductions. This team was also the pilot team for testing the benchmarking process. Faced with impending layoffs, employees of the organization made the team members the focus of attention. The pressure exerted on these people to discuss their process and investigation findings was intense. To make matters worse, the internal benchmarking specialist who trained the team videotaped each of the weekly team meetings as a process record. The results were disastrous. The team cracked under the pressure and was disbanded before reaching the halfway point of the project plan. It took almost a year for a second benchmarking effort to be launched in that organization.

The recommendation for a benchmarking team that is just starting out with its first project or two is to select an area that is relevant to the business objectives of the team and organization but is not the most complex or sensitive issue facing the organization. That way, the team can focus on learning a new process while still contributing to the achievement of business objectives.

In order to help benchmarking teams (particularly new ones) link the process with important business outcomes, Xerox asks employees to consider ten questions (see Exhibit 3-3). These questions help employees prioritize potential benchmarking projects based on need. Note that the focus of these questions includes cost reduction, problem reduction, customer satisfaction, continuous improvement, and marketplace superiority, each of which could accurately be defined as a critical success factor.

Another way to link the benchmarking process with meaningful results is to position benchmarking as a tool or technique that is complementary to a formal problem-solving process. Many organizations that use a structured approach to problem solving use benchmarking at two important stages in the problem-solving cycle: when identifying problems and when identifying solutions. First, benchmarking is useful early in the process as a team identifies problems or opportunities for improvement. By examining the best practices of other groups or organizations, employees are able to identify performance gaps or new methods for performing their work. In this case, benchmarking provides information that can help individuals or teams position their problem/opportunity statements in light of real-world improvement opportuni-

Exhibit 3-3. What to benchmark: Xerox's ten questions.

1. What is the most critical factor to my function's/organization's success (e.g., customer satisfaction, expense to revenue ratio, return on asset performance)?
2. What factors are causing the most trouble (e.g., not performing to expectations)?
3. What products or services are provided to customers?
4. What factors account for customer satisfaction?
5. What specific problems (operational) have been identified in the organization?
6. Where are the competitive pressures being felt in the organization?
7. What are the major costs (or cost "drivers") in the organization?
8. Which functions represent the highest percentage of cost?
9. Which functions have the greatest room for improvement?
10. Which functions have the greatest effect (or potential) for differentiating the organization from competitors in the marketplace?

ties. Later, benchmarking information can be useful when identifying solutions or actions in the problem-solving cycle. The benchmarking process can help expand the pool of ideas regarding what actions can be taken to address a specific problem. Other organizations that manage or confront the same types of CSFs may cooperate by providing you with ideas on how to address your particular problem or opportunity.

The integration of benchmarking with other types of total quality tools and techniques (such as problem solving) presents one of the greatest opportunities to link CSFs with meaningful business results.

"Apples to Apples": Identifying Specific CSFs

As you begin to identify the CSFs that will drive your benchmarking activity, it is important to be as specific as possible in your definitions and your metrics. This level of specificity is important at all stages of the benchmarking process, but it is extremely important during the initial stages of establishing customer requirements and planning the bench-marking project.

The reasons for specificity are easy to understand. First, a require-ment of specificity forces the benchmarking customer to consider the possible options regarding what to measure. In many cases, the bench-marking customer is too vague or general regarding the benchmarking subject. Be cautious of the benchmarking customer who is overly broad regarding benchmarking information requirements. These types of cus-tomers may indicate that they are only after a sense of the big picture or a rough comparison. However, these customers are notorious for criti-cizing benchmarking reports that omit specific benchmarking issues or measures when the benchmarking data are presented. When asked to be more specific, customers are usually able to do so.

Second, taking the time to define the specific subjects of bench-marking helps in the process of planning a measurement strategy and developing specific measures. The quality of the measures used for your benchmarking effort is in part determined by the level of detail you expect from your data-gathering efforts. Also, the level of specificity helps you to better estimate the amount of time required for benchmark-ing and the nature and numbers of people required to carry out the data-collection assignments.

Third, greater levels of specificity help your benchmark partners understand your information requirements and help them prepare information for your review. This is particularly important if you have limited access to the time and resources of your benchmark partners. Vague or general information requests often result in wasted time and effort for all parties involved in the process. Perhaps the best name for this need for specificity is the "apples-to-apples" criterion. That is, can your benchmark partners compare your measures or CSFs with their own? How much translation does an organization have to do to under-stand what you are measuring or trying to improve? The more specific and generic your CSFs, the more likely that your benchmark partners will be able to provide you with relevant information.

Three Levels of CSF Specificity

Three levels of CSF specificity are typical of most benchmarking investi-gations. When I ask benchmarkers to identify the subjects of their investigation, I usually frame the question with respect to measurement.

I find that the more specific their measures, the closer they get to an apples-to-apples dialogue with their partners. It is important to begin the process of investigation with a specific measure that allows the benchmarker to establish a common language with the benchmark partner. Then, over the course of a benchmarking discussion, the subject can expand to include more general topics related to process issues.

For example, suppose that a benchmarking team identifies billing as a CSF. Approaching a benchmark partner with a question about billing opens the discussion to a range of issues that is too broad, considering the limited amount of time that can be spent with the partner. It also allows the benchmark partner to interpret billing as it sees fit, leaving the benchmarker patiently waiting for the partner to cover the specific issues that are really the subject of interest. A subject such as billing is a level-one CSF. Adding some specificity would help focus the discussion. Suppose the subject is narrowed to billing errors. This automatically focuses the questions on a particular subset of the billing process that any benchmark partner can relate to. This is a level-two CSF. In order to get into true apples-to-apples territory, we have to identify the specific, measurable factors that define our CSF. In this case, our specific billing problems may include incorrect invoices or incorrect billing addresses. These specific billing problems can be measured quite accurately in almost any organization that tracks these kinds of billing errors. We can be even more specific and measure these types of errors over specific time periods or for specific types of products. We are now at a point where we have what I call a level-three CSF. The CSF is now defined in a way that should enable benchmark partners to respond with specific information that is directly comparable to one's own metric. In this situation, you are controlling the CSF investigation by specifying exactly what you are interested in. The benchmark partner responds according to the parameters of measurement that *you* establish. It is much easier and much more productive to start with a specific CSF and work your way into a broader discussion of process questions than it is to start with broad process issues and try to narrow the discussion to the specific areas you really need to measure.

Let's define some basic guidelines for determining whether a CSF can be classified as level one, level two, or level three (see Exhibit 3-4):

■ *Level 1.* A level-one CSF defines a broad subject area for investigation, possibly involving an organizational department or function.

Exhibit 3-4. Critical success factors: levels of specificity.

Level 1	Level 2	Level 3
Broad area or subject of investigation, usually not associated with any type of measure	Activity or process as defined by some type of aggregate measure or general functional activity	Measures of specific activities or processes
Examples	Examples	Examples
▪ Specific organizations or industry groups (computer industry)	▪ Summaries of activity levels (numbers produced or serviced)	▪ Process for reducing specific billing errors (incorrect invoices)
▪ Departments or departmental subunits (human resources, training)	▪ Key performance indicators/ratios (defect rate, sales figures, market share, billing errors)	▪ Bad debt expense as a percent of sales by product type
▪ Gross organizational activities (grievance procedures, hiring practices)		▪ Specific criteria used to assess performance for a particular job family or function
		▪ Specific technologies employed

The subject is usually too broad to involve any type of measurement. Examples: billing, the procurement process, corrective action procedures, customer satisfaction levels, marketing and promotions.

■ *Level 2.* A level-two CSF defines a more specific area of investigation than level one. A level-two CSF can often be defined by some type of aggregate measure such as number of customer complaints, number of promotions per time period, average salary levels, overall number of billing errors.

■ *Level 3.* A level-three CSF is the most specific level that can be defined, particularly by means of some type of measure or specific process description that allows your benchmark partner to produce information comparable to your own. Examples: annual budget for television advertising by market, processes for reducing scrap rates by product line, methods for determining bad debt expenses as a percent of sales.

Remember, the goal is to define CSFs as specifically as possible. If a CSF can be measured, identify a measure that will be meaningful to your benchmark partners. Strive for measures or definitions of CSFs that are unambiguous. Provide specific examples to your benchmark partners whenever possible.

Examples of CSFs

Exhibit 3-5 presents a list of actual CSFs that were identified as the subjects of completed benchmarking investigations by twenty companies experienced in benchmarking. The list breaks down the CSFs into general areas of investigation (level-one measures in bold). Under each area of investigation are examples of CSFs that border on level-two measures. This exhibit gives you a pretty good idea of typical areas of benchmarking investigation for companies that have some experience with the process.

Establishing Current Activity/Performance Levels for Your Organization

As you begin to identify CSFs and specific benchmarking metrics that are to be used in your investigation, you should also ensure that your

(*text continues on page 78*)

Exhibit 3-3. Critical success factors.

Market share
☐ By units   ☐ By dollars

Profitability
☐ Return on sales (margin)   ☐ Return on equity
☐ Return on assets

Competitor growth rates
☐ Market share by segment

Raw materials
☐ Cost as a percent of sales   ☐ Freight costs
☐ Purchase price/unit   ☐ Quality (e.g., defect rates)
☐ Yearly purchase volume   ☐ Yield (unit output per unit input)
☐ Exchange rates

Direct labor
☐ Cost as a percent of sales   ☐ Unit productivity (units produced
☐ Head count by department   per man-hour)
☐ Hourly wage rates   ☐ Revenue productivity (product
☐ Benefits rates   revenue per man-hour)
☐ Average weekly hours/   ☐ Worker demographics (age,
  worker   education level, etc.)
☐ Overtime hours
☐ Overtime rates

Indirect labor
☐ Overall cost as a percent of   ☐ Benefits rates
  sales   ☐ Exchange rates
☐ Head count by function   ☐ Unit productivity
☐ Management to direct labor   ☐ Worker demographics
☐ Salary levels

Research and development
☐ Basic R&D costs   ☐ Refinements of existing products
☐ New-product development   ☐ Cost reduction engineering
  cycle time

SAG (sales, administrative, general) costs
☐ Cost as a percent of sales   ☐ Worker demographics (age,
☐ Head count by organization   experience)
☐ Salary levels   ☐ Training costs as a percent of sales
☐ Bonus plans   ☐ Bad debt expense as a percent of
☐ Benefits plans   sales

Capital costs

- [ ] Overall asset turnover (sales/assets)
- [ ] Fixed asset turnover
- [ ] Capital expenditures as a percent of depreciation
- [ ] Depreciation rates
- [ ] Yearly lease costs
- [ ] Maintenance costs
- [ ] Inventory turnover
- [ ] Days receivable
- [ ] Days payable
- [ ] Cost of capital

Product features

- [ ] Size, shape (design)
- [ ] Styles
- [ ] Colors
- [ ] Price/pricing strategy
- [ ] Accessories (options)
- [ ] Warranties
- [ ] Guarantees

Service

- [ ] Customer complaint volume and type
- [ ] Availability of assistance
- [ ] Response time
- [ ] Mean time to repair
- [ ] Speed of delivery
- [ ] Quality of customer-contact personnel
- [ ] Order entry processes
- [ ] Availability of customer "education"

Product quality

- [ ] Production yields
- [ ] Amount of rework
- [ ] Repair expense (to company and customer)
- [ ] Mean time to product failure (reliability)
- [ ] Quality methodology (QC practices, worker involvement, statistical process control [SPC], etc.)

Image

- [ ] Customer awareness
- [ ] Levels of advertising
- [ ] Media usage
- [ ] Advertising expense
- [ ] Public perception
- [ ] Lobbying efforts
- [ ] Promotion activity
- [ ] Customer reaction to image/ advertising

Manufacturing

- [ ] Make or buy decisions
- [ ] Levels of plant "specialization"
- [ ] Hardware used for production
- [ ] Work-force skill levels
- [ ] Workplace structure (design, layout)
- [ ] Automation levels

(continues)

Exhibit 3-5 (continued).

Distribution	
☐ Channels (single/multiple)	☐ Sole distributorships or other
☐ Territory configuration	

Sales force	
☐ Size	☐ Performance levels
☐ Experience level	

Data processing/MIS	
☐ Investment in systems	☐ Applications
☐ Technology (hardware, software)	

Human resources	
☐ Sourcing/recruiting activity	☐ Affirmative action activities
☐ Compensation practices	☐ Community service activities
☐ Benefits plans	☐ Communications practices/ budgets (employee)
☐ Training activities/budgets	☐ Health and safety services
☐ Reward/recognition system	

Finance	
☐ Financial policies	☐ Debt policies
☐ Tax-related policies and strategies	☐ Dividend policies

organization has specific information regarding its own levels of activity and performance in the specified measurement areas. Otherwise, benchmarking information will have limited utility.

The level of detail, the format, and the metrics used to identify your organization's outputs or performance should be as similar as possible to the detail, format, and metrics used to assess the activities of other organizations. The importance of identifying your own level of performance is discussed further in Chapter 6.

Benchmarking Process Diagnostics

The first stage of the benchmarking process, determining what to benchmark, involves establishing customer requirements for bench-

Exhibit 3-6. The benchmarking process: Stage 1 diagnostics.

☐ The customers for the benchmarking information have been identified:
- Primary customers (users)
- Secondary customers (others who can use the information)

☐ Potential customers for benchmarking information have been sought out and contacted.

☐ The customers' requirements have been identified (see Exhibit 3-2). You (and/or members of the benchmarking team) have met personally with the benchmarking customers.

☐ A customer requirements summary has been produced and reviewed with the benchmarking customers.

☐ The benchmarking customers understand what is necessary to conduct the benchmarking investigation (e.g., time, funding, people) and are supportive of those resource requirements.

☐ Critical success factors (CSFs) have been identified:
- CSFs have been specifically defined and, when possible, converted into measures.
- CSFs have been reviewed with the benchmarking customers.

---

marking information and identifying specific critical success factors that define your areas of investigation. As you proceed through each step of the benchmarking process, you should consider your level of readiness and preparation before you proceed to the next process step. Exhibit 3-6 presents a list of statements you should consider before you move on to Stage 2 of the process. These statements allow you to diagnose your benchmarking process. If you have not complied with all the diagnostic statements, you are not ready to begin Stage 2. Consider what actions need to be taken before proceeding to the next stage. These diagnostics will be presented at the end of each chapter in Part Two—consider them carefully.

4

Stage 2: Forming a Benchmarking Team

The types of people who will perform the benchmarking activity and the numbers of people involved are fairly broad issues that need to be addressed early by organizations establishing an organized and structured benchmarking process. Why is it important to identify who will benchmark this early in the process? The answer is simple. As soon as the customer requirements for benchmarking are known, the actual process of benchmarking can begin. As you will discover (if you haven't already), the planning, organization, and deployment of a well-designed benchmarking investigation involves a considerable amount of time and energy. Engaging reinforcements to share the work load and developing an equitable division of labor are not only practical considerations, in most cases they are required. Also, by identifying a qualified and motivated team of benchmarkers early in the process, you can take advantage of the group's diverse experiences, professional affiliations, and individual interests.

Benchmarking as a Team Activity

Why use the word *team* (see Exhibit 4-1)? Can't benchmarking be done by individuals? The answer is yes. However, the rallying cry for the formation of benchmarking teams should be "Remember the work load!" The amount of work alone justifies the involvement of a team. However, there are other reasons benchmarking is an appropriate team

Exhibit 4-1. The benchmarking process: Stage

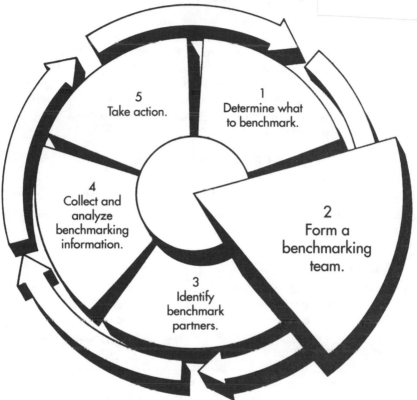

activity. Remember, in many benchmarking investigations, a group of employees can designate itself as the primary customer (or user) of benchmarking information. These employees are the primary beneficiaries of the benchmarking process, and they are responsible for implementing changes based, in part, on the results of their benchmarking. These groups of employees are usually motivated to participate in the benchmarking investigation and to make it both thorough and meaningful. Another good reason for the use of teams is the level of functional expertise and work experience a team represents. Different perspectives, special skills, variety of business connections, physical location—

these are the dimensions that individual team members bring to the benchmarking process.

Why use the word *team* instead of *group*? This is an important distinction. *Group* merely signifies numbers, that is, more than one. There are no performance implications in the word *group*. However, the word *team* introduces quite a few expectations regarding the behavior of a group, such as common purpose or goal, coordination, cooperation, communication, and motivation. These are the attributes that separate teams from groups. For benchmarking, you definitely want a team.

Types of Benchmarking Teams

In general, there are three basic types of benchmarking teams as defined by their structure and reporting relationships.

Intact Work Groups

The first type of team is the intact work group. This group is usually in a single location with all members of the group reporting to a common manager. In these groups, the manager may or may not assume the role of the benchmarking team leader (this role is discussed later in this chapter). Usually every member of the work group participates as a benchmarking team member. However, in large groups the number of benchmarkers may be limited, depending on the scope of the project and the work load of the various group members.

Intact work groups are often the customers for their own benchmarking investigations. This is due to the integration of benchmarking with other tools and techniques, such as structured problem solving. One benefit of this situation is that the team does not need to get outside approvals in order to proceed with the process. Also, the team can make adjustments in its own requirements or objectives based on the information that is produced as the investigation progresses. In most cases, these types of teams are likely to regard benchmarking as a continuous process that exceeds the scope of any one particular investigation or project.

Cross-Functional, Interdepartmental, and Interorganizational Teams

These teams are often structured as task teams or task forces with specific charters and defined sets of customers who are usually commissioning managers. The individuals selected for these teams are chosen for their specific knowledge or skill levels, but they also act as representatives of their respective departments, locations, or divisions. The leader or project manager of these types of teams is usually not the everyday manager of most team members.

In many cases, these types of teams are brought together to work on one specific issue or problem. Once their benchmarking investigation is complete, the team disbands. There are some situations, however, in which such a team would be expected to conduct investigations on a more periodic basis. For example, groups of functional specialists (e.g., training managers, computer programmers, transportation specialists) may conduct a joint benchmarking project on a periodic (e.g., annual) basis in order to gauge the state-of-the-art business practices in their functional areas and to recommend any action that may improve their outputs or work processes.

These types of teams often produce recommendations or reports and present those findings to their sponsors or to upper management. In some cases, these teams are empowered to make changes, but in most cases their assignment is to conduct an investigation and then make recommendations.

Ad Hoc Teams

This type of team represents the ultimate in team flexibility. An ad hoc team can consist of any number of employees who share common interests or responsibilities and decide that a benchmarking investigation on some subject is warranted. An ad hoc team can be called together by an individual, or it can be formed as the result of a team decision. Usually the ad hoc team defines a specific subject for benchmarking and continues to function until the benchmarking investigation is complete. This type of team may be made up of managers or nonmanagers—any employee or group of employees that has identified a need for benchmarking information. The role of team leader or project manager is often decided by the team or is assumed by the person who initiated the team activity.

In mature benchmarking companies (e.g., Xerox, Motorola, Milliken), the ability to form ad hoc benchmarking teams is greatly enhanced due to the overall levels of process awareness, process support, and actual hands-on experience with benchmarking. These organizations have created an environment in which this type of activity and initiative is encouraged and rewarded. Thus, employees are likely to look for opportunities to apply benchmarking to any situation that might warrant investigation. For organizations just beginning to benchmark, it may take a few years of benchmarking experience before ad hoc benchmarking teams become a reality.

Who Is Involved in the Benchmarking Process?

Before we get into the actual structure and the roles and responsibilities of benchmarking teams, it is important to identify, from a broader perspective, the people who participate in the benchmarking process and are responsible for maintaining benchmarking from an overall organizational standpoint. When you contact another organization with a benchmarking request, these are the types of people you are likely to come in contact with. If you are just beginning to introduce benchmarking in your organization, these are the people you might need to help you start up, maintain, and expand your benchmarking activities.

Internal Benchmarking Specialists

Benchmarking specialists are employees of the organization who have been trained in the process of benchmarking and whose normal work responsibilities include benchmarking-related tasks. These specialists may be staff employees (e.g., quality specialists) or they may be from the line organization (e.g., manufacturing or engineering managers). The amount of time they dedicate to benchmarking activities may vary from 25 percent to 100 percent. In some cases, these specialists serve a coordinating or executive function and direct the benchmarking efforts of employees who perform the bulk of the benchmarking assignments.

In larger organizations with established benchmarking histories, benchmarking specialists usually have the word *benchmarking* in their job titles. In some cases these individuals are associated with the quality function or the training and development department. In other organizations, such as AT&T, an internal benchmarking consulting group may work at the corporate level. In smaller organizations, or in organizations just beginning to establish the benchmarking process, there may be one or two individuals who have been given responsibility for initiating the process. This is likely to be a part-time assignment as the organization gains more awareness of the process implications and/or demonstrates the process by launching a benchmarking pilot project. In small organizations, the person or persons responsible for benchmarking are likely to wear other hats as well. Over time, benchmarking responsibilities and activities may increase and could require a full-time assignment.

Benchmarking specialists are often assigned by functional area. For example, in large organizations there may be benchmarking specialists for manufacturing, engineering, finance, human resources, marketing, and so on. In most cases, the benchmarking assignment is a part-time job for these functional specialists. There are advantages to this type of specialization. First, specialists are familiar with the benchmarking process and the history of its use in their functional areas. There is no need for specialists to get "up to speed" in an area in which they have no experience or knowledge. Second, as benchmarking projects are initiated over time, functional specialists have already begun the process of establishing benchmarking networks among functional professionals in their areas of expertise. These networks can greatly enhance the efficiency and effectiveness of the benchmarking process.

Benchmarking specialists can also be found in individual divisions or geographical locations of organizations. These people are usually responsible for the benchmarking activities at a particular site. These specialists may be part of a formal or informal benchmarking network, the hub of which is usually at the corporate level. There are instances in decentralized organizations in which the introduction and development of a number of benchmarking departments have taken place without any planning, organization, or cooperation among the various operating units. This may result in an organization having a variety of benchmarking processes within its component divisions. In such a situation, there may be some differences in the benchmarking models and processes used, the relative positioning and use of the benchmarking process itself, and how benchmarking information is gathered and used. One way for organizations to coordinate these decentralized activities is through the formation of internal quality councils or networks. These groups provide a forum for benchmarkers representing different organizational locations, divisions, or functional specialties to gather and share information and experiences. These internal networks provide opportunities for information sharing, coordination of efforts, joint projects, and the elimination of redundant benchmarking efforts.

In general, the responsibilities of benchmarking specialists focus in three major areas. Benchmarking specialists may be involved in one or more of these areas as required by their organizations.

1. *Organizing and managing the benchmarking process.* On a macro level, these responsibilities may include finding benchmarking process resources (e.g., trainers, consultants) and introducing quality tools and processes into the organization. Process specialists may develop an overall benchmarking strategy or plan—a blueprint for the use of benchmarking in their organizations or functions. These specialists may also be responsible for educating or orienting employees (from top management down) on the definition of and potential applications for benchmarking. These people may also be responsible for staffing the benchmarking network, including the hiring and training of other benchmarkers (or hiring someone to do the job). Internal specialists are often responsible for establishing and maintaining a benchmarking database or filing system to ensure that the work of benchmarking teams is recorded for presentation and reporting purposes and to stimulate the use of the information by other employees in the organization. Benchmarking specialists are also usually responsible for assessing the state of the process and periodically reporting the status of benchmarking activities to senior management.

On a micro level, internal specialists often work directly with benchmarking teams. Their responsibilities might include establishing the customer requirements for the benchmarking activity, selecting and briefing the benchmarking team, and serving as a project manager. In some cases, they may also serve as process facilitators ensuring that employees or consultants are adhering to the prescribed benchmarking processes and are producing a product that will meet their customer's requirements. Their responsibilities may also include the production and presentation of benchmarking reports with or for teams.

2. *Training.* Benchmarking specialists may provide training to employees on managing and conducting the benchmarking process on either a regularly scheduled basis (i.e., offering classes on a regular schedule) or an as-needed basis. They may also serve as master trainers and provide train-the-trainer services for their organizations or departments. At DEC, internal benchmarking specialists (full-time) have produced over 200 qualified facilitators in train-the-trainer sessions. They have also trained at least five master trainers who are qualified to train other trainers.

3. *Benchmarking.* Specialists may be involved in the actual process of benchmarking—working with benchmarking customers, planning benchmarking activities, gathering and analyzing data, and so on. In

other words, benchmarking specialists can also be regular members of benchmarking teams.

External Benchmarking Specialists

Benchmarking specialists from outside the organization are typically consultants who specialize in various aspects of the benchmarking process. In many situations, organizations use these specialists during the start-up phase of the benchmarking process. As the internal level of expertise grows, the outside specialists are gradually withdrawn, returning to provide occasional special services on an as-needed basis. External benchmarking specialists can perform a variety of services, and they often develop areas of specialization or competence. There are several types of specialists who can help organizations manage their benchmarking processes.

The first type of consultant specializes in planning benchmarking projects, training employees in basic benchmarking processes, directing benchmarking projects, and producing reports. These consultants are usually under contract to a middle- or senior-level manager and are accountable during the benchmarking process to the contracting manager. In this situation, the organization's employees actually perform the bulk of the benchmarking tasks, but they do so under the direction of the consultant.

The second type of consultant provides specialized support services such as training or facilitation support. Often these consultants are specialized in particular functional areas (e.g., engineering, manufacturing, finance) or industries (e.g., automotive, food products). Some companies, such as DEC and Xerox, use external specialists to collect benchmarking information from competitors, particularly when sensitive issues are involved. These specialists are experienced in initiating communications with competitive companies and add an air of impartiality to the benchmarking activities. In some competitive benchmarking situations, these consultants produce what are referred to as "blind reports." These reports conceal the identities of the benchmark partners when the final results are delivered to the participants. Each organization that participates receives a report that identifies the partner companies by using a neutral code such as a numerical designation.

The third type of consultant manages an entire benchmarking project from start to finish. In this case, employees are generally not used in the benchmarking process or are used to perform specific assignments under the direction of the consultant. The product provided by the consultant in this case is the benchmarking service plus the production of a report, which may vary in level of detail and analysis. Because of the costs involved, this level of external participation is usually limited to projects under the direction of senior management (or a manager with an extremely healthy budget).

A relatively new service being provided by consultants is help in locating best-practices companies. In most cases, consulting firms or research consortia (e.g., the American Productivity and Quality Center—APQC) conduct some type of analysis or survey to identify best-practices organizations by industry type or functional area. These lists of best-practices companies are available for a fee or are provided to members and "friends" of the consortium. When using such lists, be sure to investigate the methods these organizations use to identify best practices, and avoid an overdependence on these types of referrals.

Employees

Most benchmarking projects use employees to help plan, conduct, analyze, and present benchmarking efforts. The level of involvement of employees may vary from basic data-collection and analysis tasks to project planning and management assignments. At one extreme, employees are selected to participate as part of a benchmarking team. They are trained in basic benchmarking skills, presented with a project plan, and directed in their activities by a project manager or benchmarking specialist. This is most often a short-term assignment, and the employee is not expected to continue to engage in additional benchmarking activities once the basic project is completed.

In other situations, however, large numbers of employees are trained in benchmarking skills and are expected (on their own initiative) to generate local benchmarking projects or participate in local benchmarking activities. In many cases, these employees are the customers for their own benchmarking efforts. In these organizations, benchmarking becomes an expected behavior, and benchmarking projects are conducted on a continual basis. This situation is typical of a mature benchmarking process and is often identified as the desired state by organizations that are new to benchmarking.

The Benchmarking Team: Roles and Responsibilities

There are several major areas of responsibility associated with a benchmarking team effort. Each of these roles is important to the eventual

Exhibit 4-2. A typical benchmarking team structure.

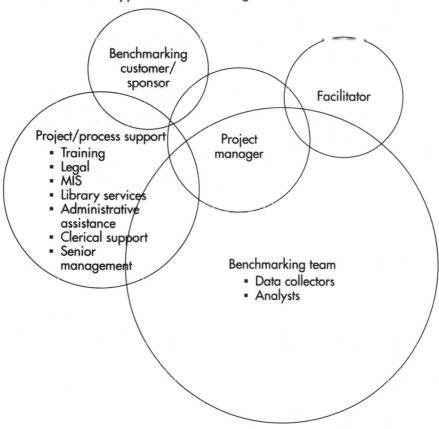

success of the benchmarking project. In most benchmarking organizations, there is a fairly common core team structure. These are the employees who perform the majority of the benchmarking tasks. In addition to this core, there are a variety of other employees or external specialists who can provide specific services to the team on an as-needed basis. The team structure must allow these specialists or project support people to enter and exit the team with a high degree of ease and flexibility.

Exhibit 4-2 is a diagram of a typical benchmarking team structure.

The basic structure is depicted as a set of intersecting circles that demonstrates the flexibility of the team structure and conveys the idea that these team structures do not necessarily conform to traditional structures and reporting relationships. Note the relationship between the project manager and the customer/sponsor. Although the project manager is the key interface between the team and the customer, there may not be a formal reporting relationship involved. Thus, a traditional organization chart would not be appropriate to demonstrate this particular set of relationships. Also note that the facilitator and the project/process support staff are outside the core team. This implies that these specialists can be called on to participate in team activities as needed. By maintaining this type of relationship with benchmarking teams, facilitators and specialists are able to support many teams simultaneously.

Project Manager

The project manager is responsible for planning and organizing the benchmarking activities for the team. This individual is the primary contact with the benchmarking customer or sponsor. The project manager is also charged with maintaining basic benchmarking process discipline—the "keeper of the process," so to speak. The project manager, as the name implies, is responsible for the basic tasks that are required to manage the team (for a list of specific team member roles, responsibilities, and skill levels, see Exhibit 4-3). The project manager also serves as a link between the team and other benchmarking resources or teams throughout the organization. In some organizations, the project manager is even responsible for training the members of the benchmarking team.

In many cases, the project manager is the natural leader or manager of the benchmarking team. He or she may also be the most senior person on a cross-functional or cross-divisional team. However, most teams are flexible about assigning a team leader. It is common for team members to elect a team leader. In other cases, the senior manager delegates the project manager assignment to another member of the team. Some teams rotate the project manager assignment. In companies such as Xerox and Motorola, any of the situations just described (or combinations thereof) can be found throughout their organizations.

Regardless of the specific individual who assumes the role of project manager, there are several skills and traits that characterize that posi-

Exhibit 4-3. Benchmarking role profiles.

Role	Responsibilities	Skills
Project manager ▪ Plan, organize, staff, direct, and control the benchmarking project. Link the results with other organizational units.	▪ Identify customers and their requirements. ▪ Select members of benchmarking team. ▪ Develop and monitor budget. ▪ Select outside suppliers/consultants. ▪ Consider legal, ethical project issues. ▪ Provide project briefings. ▪ Monitor project progress. ▪ Negotiate commitments with benchmark partners. ▪ Negotiate commitments from internal and external resources. ▪ Communicate/present results of project to necessary target audience. ▪ Manage group discussions and group processes. ▪ Provide benchmarking training.	▪ Communications (speaking, listening) ▪ Writing ▪ Negotiating ▪ Planning ▪ Organizing ▪ Delegating ▪ Presentation ▪ Political ▪ Leadership ▪ Group dynamics
Data collector/analyst ▪ Develop and use benchmarking techniques to collect, analyze, and present data.	▪ Assist in development of project plan. ▪ Design and produce data-collection instruments. ▪ Schedule appointments with data sources. ▪ Gather data. ▪ Summarize data. ▪ Analyze data. ▪ Identify performance gaps. ▪ Present results. ▪ Produce summary reports.	▪ Planning ▪ Organizing ▪ Communications (speaking, listening) ▪ Interviewing ▪ Writing ▪ Interpersonal
Benchmarking project support ▪ Provide support to benchmarking team as required.	▪ Facilitation ▪ Training ▪ Document processing ▪ Graphics support ▪ Legal counsel ▪ Computer support ▪ Database management ▪ Library services	▪ Communications ▪ Interpersonal ▪ Professional

tion. First, the person should be well schooled in the benchmarking process—familiar with each of the process stages and the specific tasks required at each stage, and able to communicate this information to others. Second, the individual must possess excellent project management skills such as planning, organizing, scheduling, and coordinating. Third, the project manager has to be able to work within the organizational system in order to acquire resources and support for the team. Given these demanding responsibilities, many teams split the project management assignments among two or three team members.

Data Collector/Analyst

The data collectors and analysts are the true core of the benchmarking team. These are the people who assist in the development of the benchmarking plan; identify, contact, and interview benchmark partners; analyze and summarize the benchmarking data; and produce benchmarking reports. These are the true "worker bees" of the benchmarking process.

Data collectors do not necessarily have to be benchmarking experts, nor do they have to be expert process facilitators. Their primary responsibility is to act under the direction of the project manager. As a long-term developmental goal, you would like to have all benchmarkers develop their expertise so that any member of the team could be project manager or process facilitator. However, for most teams using the process for the first time (or during the first few project cycles), the activities of the data collectors or core team members are somewhat limited.

In some benchmarking projects, large quantities of information are collected by the benchmarking team. In these situations, many benchmarking teams designate a number of individuals (usually one or two) to be information analysts. Their primary responsibility is to summarize all the information collected by the benchmarking team. This may take the form of transferring information onto summary forms or writing summary narratives based on the information submitted by the team members. Some assignments might include setting up spreadsheets and other computerized systems for summarizing and analyzing data in some type of matrix format. In some cases, analysts do not engage in routine data-collection activities (e.g., interviewing benchmark partners) but specialize in the information-summarizing tasks and avoid benchmarking "roadwork" whenever possible.

Benchmarking Project Support

The typical benchmarking team requires some level of support during the course of the investigation. This support usually involves a specific service or expert opinion that enables the team to complete its assignments with maximum effectiveness. This is where the team needs to be flexible in terms of its ability and willingness to use outside support. Teams that establish good working relationships with these support personnel and are able to secure the assistance they need with a minimum of disruption are more productive and produce better-quality outputs. The most frequently needed project support resources are listed here (in no particular order of importance).

Facilitation

Process facilitation support is often required for new teams or for teams that are dealing with controversial or sensitive subjects. In some organizations, such as AT&T, full-time benchmarking support staff is available to any team that requests it. In other organizations, facilitation support may be available from other experienced benchmarkers who volunteer to help teams with their process needs. Consultants can also be called in to provide special facilitation support or to perform a process check in order to help a team diagnose areas for process improvement.

Training

Training support may be required for new teams or for teams that have added new members. This training can range from a ground-up introduction to benchmarking to specialized instruction on some aspect of the benchmarking process (e.g., data-collection tools, interviewing skills).

Legal

If a benchmarking team is dealing with a sensitive issue that may involve proprietary or sensitive information, or if there are antitrust questions, then the team should review its questions with the organization's legal counsel. In some organizations, every benchmarking investigation involves a trip to the attorney's office for approval or review of the benchmarking subjects. Other organizations avoid legal review and approach counsel only if the benchmarking subject seems obviously sensitive or proprietary.

Management Information Systems (MIS)

The MIS function can help a team when the benchmarking information calls for a spreadsheet analysis or summary. MIS specialists can develop customized spreadsheets and educate team members regarding proper information entry procedures. Also, the MIS function can be helpful in establishing a benchmarking database. This benchmarking database can be designed to provide the general employee population with access to the results of benchmarking results via remote terminals.

Library Services

Internal library services (also called technical libraries or research libraries) provide invaluable support to benchmarking teams that are investigating printed information. Professional libraries provide excellent support by conducting literature searches and locating periodicals, directories, analyst reports, books, databases, foreign information sources, and so on. Many large companies use their internal library and research resources extensively and have their internal benchmarking specialists serve as links between the benchmarking teams and research staffs. The specialist's job is to consolidate information requests and act as a buffer between the variety of teams in the workplace and the researchers.

Organizations that do not have internal research support or libraries can obtain the same type of library support services from large public libraries or the libraries of local universities or colleges. It is advisable to contact these libraries and become acquainted with the types of services they offer and the fees they charge.

Administrative Assistance and Clerical Support

Benchmarking teams often require administrative assistance and clerical support for a variety of tasks, including word processing, forms creation, filing, and telephone assistance (e.g., setting appointments, receiving calls from benchmark partners). In many situations, the benchmarking work is added to the normal work load of everyone involved, including administrative assistants who report to benchmarking employees or administrative assistants who are themselves members of benchmarking teams. The objective is to plan ahead and keep the support staff advised of impending work loads.

Senior Management

Although not normally relegated to the category of project support, senior staff members are often called upon for assistance. In most cases, the need is for additional resource support in the form of time, funding, or people. In other situations, access to normally restricted information might be needed. Or a team might need communications support from senior management in the form of official letters or phone calls to benchmark partners to provide some additional clout to the team's request for information. Finally, as the benchmarking team moves into the "take action" stage of the benchmarking process, senior management may be called upon to lend support by providing the resources necessary for the team or organization to take action.

Skills and Attributes of an Effective Benchmarker

What skills and attributes characterize an effective benchmarker? Should everyone be a benchmarker, or should you be cautious when selecting the members of your benchmarking team? These are commonly asked questions in organizations that are new to benchmarking, particularly in situations in which pilot benchmarking projects will be commissioned in order to observe the process. The answer to these questions is that there are some explicit qualifications for benchmarking team members that should be considered before launching a benchmarking team. The criteria proposed in this section provide guidelines to help make effective choices. For organizations that are restricted (mostly by size) in the choices they can make, it is still wise to consider these attributes and attempt to maximize the effectiveness of those choices that are available.

It should be noted that a desirable objective for any organization is to have every employee trained and ready to be an effective benchmarker. In fact, many organizations have specific goals to do just that. The power of benchmarking is certainly an inducement to maximize the number of people qualified to lead and participate in the process. However, it is advisable to demonstrate the process in its early stages with benchmarkers who can serve as role models for those who will follow.

Ability: The "Can Do" Factor

Individual benchmarkers should have some basic skills and abilities. The exact level of these abilities needs to be defined in each organization. Four specific characteristics should be considered essential benchmarking credentials.

1. *Functional expertise.* Successful benchmarkers should be proficient in their areas of functional specialization. They should demonstrate an acceptable level of job skills and work-related performance as defined by the organization. These individuals do not necessarily need to be the best and brightest, but they should be above-average performers. This is important for several reasons. First, these benchmarkers represent opportunities for organizational improvement; they will be making recommendations and taking actions that may change the way the organization conducts business; they must be able to make distinctions between useful (i.e., an improvement opportunity) and nonuseful information. Second, these individuals will be representing the organization as they make contact with benchmark partners. It is preferable for these benchmarking "ambassadors" to represent an organization's best practices. After all, will a below-average performer be able to adequately investigate best practices in another organizational environment? Do you want to take that chance?

A warning: Do not use the benchmarking process as an opportunity to give marginal performers a learning experience. The benchmarking process is one of discovery, but it is not a learning laboratory for below-average or marginal performers.

2. *Credibility.* Functional expertise is, in itself, not a sufficient qualification for a benchmarker. An individual employee needs to have a certain amount of credibility within his or her own organization as well as with the benchmark partners. Credibility is often judged by subject-matter knowledge, work history, and organizational position. Individuals who are not credible among their peers, employees, or managers will have limited impact when making recommendations based on their benchmarking investigations. The results of even the most rigorous benchmarking investigation will be questioned if the employees conducting that investigation are not considered credible.

Employees who are respected in their organizations tend to be opinion leaders. These people often make the best candidates for benchmarkers; their work will not be challenged on the basis of personal credibility or trust.

3. *Communications skills.* One of the key skills of an effective benchmarker is the ability to communicate. Even the most credible functional experts won't be successful benchmarkers if they can't communicate with other members of the benchmarking team or, more importantly, with the benchmark partners. This skill includes written communications but refers more to verbal abilities. The ability to plan and organize a benchmarking investigation will be offset by an inability to communicate these plans and objectives to others. Likewise, subject knowledge is of little value if it can't be explained or questions can't be asked or answered effectively.

I attended a presentation made by a group of eleven engineers who had been working for seven months as a benchmarking pilot team. The team was making its final report to the senior staff of a division of a large aerospace company in southern California. The senior staff had been given a briefing book several days prior to the presentation that summarized the team's activities. The report was quite impressive. The team had demonstrated an effective use of the benchmarking process, and its methods for collecting and analyzing data were imaginative and productive. I anticipated an outstanding presentation. However, when I heard the presentation, I couldn't believe that these were the same team members who produced the report. The description of their process was confusing, their methodology discussion was reduced to a two-minute summary, and they failed to respond directly to the questions that were posed at the conclusion of their presentation. In short, their verbal communications skills lapsed in front of this audience and almost cost them an endorsement of their findings by senior staff. I wondered how they were able to communicate so effectively with their benchmark partners. I approached the team leader and asked him that question. He said, "That part was easy—they were engineers!"

4. *Team spirit.* In addition to the attributes listed earlier, effective benchmarkers need to be able to function as members of a team. Individuals who have a reputation for being difficult to work with in group situations may present problems on a benchmarking team. Attributes of team players include a spirit of cooperation, effective listening skills, an ability to reach a consensus, and respect for the opinions of others.

Motivation: The "Want to" Factor

All the ability in the world won't make a bit of difference if an individual does not want to perform as a member of a benchmarking team. In fact, highly expert and credible opinion leaders can be a major detriment to a team if they are constantly complaining about their lack of interest in the team activity or their lack of time to participate. In most cases, it is better to have a benchmarking team member who has average abilities but is highly motivated than it is to have an individual who has outstanding abilities but poor motivation.

Some organizations have attempted to manage the low motivation factor and have demonstrated positive results. One method is to engage the poorly motivated individual as a special functional consultant who can be called into the group to supply special expertise as needed (e.g., reviewing CSF measures, identifying best practices). Poorly motivated individuals often respond positively to this role, but the project manager should follow up on any assignments to ensure that this person fulfills his or her obligations to the team.

Another technique that has worked for some organizations is to select a group of more than enough potential benchmarkers who fit the ability criteria. This group is then presented with an overview of the benchmarking assignment, including projected work load, a summary of the customer requirements (if available), and a request for volunteers to step forward based on a desire to participate. At this point, individuals self-select in or out of the team based on the motivation factor. This strategy helps some organizations produce a balanced combination of ability and motivation.

Selection Criteria to Avoid

There are three selection criteria that should be avoided as you go about the task of identifying potential benchmarking team members.

1. *Convenience.* Individuals who are selected on this basis may be logical choices because they are positioned conveniently within the organizational system. The convenience may be attributable to their physical location in the organization (George is a mechanical engineer, and he happens to be located in New Britain) or their functional or organizational affiliation (Pat is from design and engineering, and we need a representative from D&E to balance the team).

2. *Availability*. In this case, individuals are usually in a work lull and appear to have time available, or they are available because of a lack of work in their assignment area.

3. *Expendability*. The organization can manage quite well without these types of people. Neither their skills nor their time on the job is very important to the organization's success.

Basing your selection of benchmarking team members on these types of criteria reduces the effectiveness of the team and could possibly result in a stigma being attached to the benchmarking assignment. If your organization puts out a call for benchmarking team members, make sure that the attributes of a desirable team member are explicitly identified in the membership posting.

Benchmarking Training

Most benchmarking organizations offer formal training to employees who will be using the benchmarking process. This training is usually tailored to the organization's information requirements, benchmarking philosophy, and specific benchmarking model. The following training-related issues should be considered as an organization prepares to launch its first benchmarking project.

The Basic Curriculum

Most best-practices benchmarkers, including Xerox and AT&T, offer two basic benchmarking courses: a one- or two-day basic skills course and a two- to four-hour management briefing session. The subjects covered in one- or two-day basic skills courses include the following:

- An overview of the benchmarking process
- A statement of the intended uses and applications of benchmarking in the organization
- A review of basic terms and tools that are common to benchmarking
- A review of the roles and responsibilities of benchmarking team members

- A section on data-collection methods (e.g., interviewing techniques, information searches, survey construction)
- Recommended benchmarking protocols (e.g., making effective and professional contact with benchmark partners)
- A brief review of ethical issues concerning benchmarking
- Basic project management tools and techniques

Additional training is often offered. For example, DEC offers a three-day train-the-trainer course that includes modules on human relations and communications skills. Xerox offers a one-day televised workshop that can be accessed by students, suppliers, customers, and the general public through colleges and training centers. Other types of training involve facilitation skills and information-gathering and analysis skills such as interviewing and survey construction.

Features of the Training Process

Who Trains?

Most benchmarking training is provided internally, either by full- or part-time benchmarking experts or through the traditional training department or quality organization. Most organizations use a small number of content experts as internal training resources. DEC's three-day train-the-trainer program is an attempt to increase this internal trainer pool.

Some organizations use outside consultants to train, but usually only in the initial stages of setting up a training program. Most organizations then transfer the training activity to their internal staff. At this juncture, consultants often provide train-the-trainer support and co-train with internal staff to get them up to speed. Some of the large industry group consortia offer benchmarking training as part of their cooperative effort to train members in total quality management skills. This spreads the cost of benchmarking training to a larger customer base and encourages consortium members to begin the communication process and actual benchmarking. Some organizations use generic benchmarking training that is provided by their customers or suppliers. Motorola makes benchmarking training available to its customer and supplier base. DEC supplies training to its customers to complement its products and services; it does not intend to earn a profit from this benchmarking training.

Who Is Trained?

There is a preference for training only benchmarking team members who are ready to conduct a benchmarking investigation. Xerox, for instance, used to encourage all employees to attend benchmarking training sessions whether they had a benchmarking project or not. Recently, however, the model for training has become more of an on-the-job format for teams that are actively pursuing a benchmarking investigation. The result is fewer traditional classroom classes and more classes being conducted in the field. DEC uses a similar training format and is conducting "focused" training for benchmarking teams that involves tailoring the training content for individual teams. The key word for DEC is *flexibility* regarding the training content, format, and audience. IBM's goal is not to train everybody in the benchmarking process but to offer the training as demand dictates—the demand being determined by the number of new projects and project teams being formed.

The Preliminary Project Calendar

As soon as a benchmarking team is identified, the project manager should immediately begin applying basic project management techniques in order to ensure that the team's activities and assignments are clearly identified and understood by the members of the team and others with a need to know. Planning and organizing are critical to a benchmarking team's effectiveness and efficiency, especially when the team consists of individuals who are not members of an intact work group. In many task team situations, members of a benchmarking team get together only on a weekly or monthly basis. Between meetings team members pursue their own assignments and must manage their own benchmarking activity schedules. Unfortunately, there are numerous opportunities for assignments to fall between the cracks or for individuals to forget assignments. In order to ensure that all project assignments are completed thoroughly and on time, the project manager should make use of proven time management tools.

In order to prepare the team for the project planning discussions and the various benchmarking tasks that will follow, the project manager should prepare a preliminary project calendar that identifies key tasks or assignments, the person or persons responsible for each task, and the expected completion dates (with key interim reporting dates

Exhibit 4-4. Benchmarking project planning calendar.

Task	Assignment	Notes	1	2	3	4	5	6
1. Establish customer requirements.	Alex Smith	Meeting scheduled with senior marketing staff, July 1.		▲				
2. Select benchmarking team.	Alex Smith	Engineering team only; solicit input from senior staff.		▲				
3. Hold team briefing.	Alex Smith	Arrange off-site meeting.			▲			
4. Develop project plan.	Benchmarking team				△	▲		
5. Collect data and perform analysis.	Benchmarking team	Interim reports every two weeks.				△△△△	▲	
6. Present benchmarking report.	Benchmarking team and presentation leader (TBA)	Report to senior staff prior to November 26.						▲

Six-Month Calendar

△ Interim report
▲ Task completed
— Ongoing

Exhibit 4-5. The benchmarking process: Stage 2 diagnostics.

☐ The organization has identified the types of benchmarking teams that will be organized and supported during the initial stages of process implementation (e.g., intact work teams, task teams, ad hoc teams). The definitions of these team structures are known within the organization.

☐ The organization has allocated sufficient resources to support the start-up of benchmarking teams (e.g., time, funding, process support).

☐ Internal benchmarking specialists have been identified, trained, and oriented regarding their roles in supporting the benchmarking process.

☐ Senior management has been briefed regarding its role in supporting the benchmarking efforts of employees.

☐ Benchmarking team members have been selected based on the criteria of ability and motivation.

☐ Benchmarking project support staff have been briefed regarding their likely roles in the support of benchmarking activities.

☐ Project planning tools (e.g., project planning calendars) are available to assist benchmarking teams. Team members have been trained to use effective project management techniques.

noted). Exhibit 4-4 illustrates an example of a benchmarking project planning calendar. This type of calendar is similar to PERT charts, Gantt charts, responsibility charts, and other common project planning tools. This first-draft calendar helps establish realistic objectives and gives team members an indication of how their personal calendars will be affected for the life of the project. This type of calendar should be distributed to all employees or groups that are affected (or potentially affected) by the benchmarking activity, especially those individuals who are likely to become involved with the team as project support staff.

Regardless of the types of project planning tools used in your organization, it is important that all benchmarking assignments be stated clearly and be understood by those with a need to know. It is advisable to establish this calendar as soon as possible with members of the team. Team members should also be instructed to inform the project manager of any problems or changes associated with their assignments as soon as possible so that adjustments in the project planning calendar can be made and other team members can be notified of the changes.

Consider the basic diagnostic indicators in Exhibit 4-5 before you move on to the next step of the benchmarking process.

5

Stage 3: Identifying
Benchmark Partners

Stage 3 of the benchmarking process involves the identification of benchmark partners (see Exhibit 5-1). My definition of a benchmark partner is any person or organization that supplies you with information related to your benchmarking investigation. This is a rather broad definition, but it is intended to open the door to all sorts of information possibilities. The term *partner* implies (using the basic dictionary definition) "one who is an ally" or "one who enters into an association" with you. This is a very different perspective on data collection than the traditional competitive analysis model, which treats the objects of your information search, particularly competitors, as antagonists, or worse, as enemies. Organizations that have taken this partnering approach report high levels of cooperation and positive results with the organizations they have contacted. A direct person-to-person approach when dealing with functional counterparts has yielded dividends in the form of improved levels of information quantity and quality.

The focus of this chapter is on information: information from people—employees (internal and external), experts, analysts, researchers, consultants—and information from organizations—your organization, other organizations, the government, research groups, universities, trade and professional associations, and so on. All of these resources are potential benchmark partners.

The Objective: Your Own Benchmarking Information Network

Think about information as a resource, something you can use as a tool to improve your decision-making process. Think about the long term,

Exhibit 5-1. The benchmarking process: Stage 3.

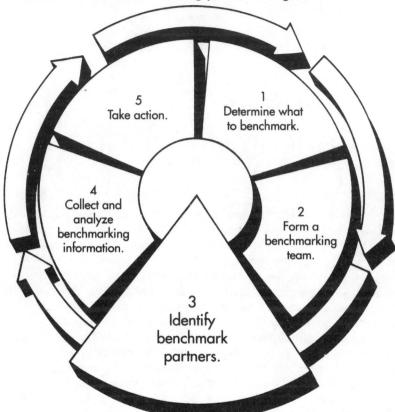

as implied by the terms *relationships* and *partnerships*. Consider the concept of an intelligence network. Think about the process of collecting information as well as the information itself. These ideas and concepts represent the frame of mind that one should have when thinking about benchmarking.

Certainly, information consists of facts, numbers, trendlines, process descriptions, even observations. However, the usefulness of these pieces of information is lost over time. The half-life of many facts and numbers can be counted in weeks or months. After collecting an information set made up of facts, a decision maker has a limited period of time in which he or she can use that information to make a reasonable decision. On the other hand, the process of collecting information and tapping the sources of useful information may be much more stable and reliable over time. For example, the facts that are collected out of a particular reference document (e.g., a directory, product manual, electronic database) may have limited utility based on the specific subject being investigated and the time frame available to make a decision. The actual reference documents, however, have a greater long-term utility based on their accuracy, ease of use, and accessibility. The same can be said for people. You can obtain information from a person who offers expertise and experience by asking specific questions over the telephone. Although the information you collect fills a specific short-term need, that person represents a potential resource that could be useful to you in many similar situations over a much longer period of time.

The reference documents and the individuals you use to collect benchmarking information should be considered potential long-term resources. Those resources that have produced useful and reliable information over time can become part of your benchmarking information network. This network may eventually evolve to the point where you can locate the information you need with a high degree of efficiency if you take advantage of the opportunity to develop an information network geared toward your needs.

There are several advantages to forming your own benchmarking information network. First, you can narrow your list of contacts down to those that have established a history of providing reliable information. Second, the amount of time spent tracking information leads can be greatly decreased. Third, as your information needs change based on the subject or scope of your benchmarking project, you won't have to begin your information search from scratch—your information network is the automatic starting point for any benchmarking activity. At the same time, other individuals and benchmarking teams are developing their own information networks that reflect their project focus or functional specialization. These people and teams can be valuable resources if you take advantage of their networking activities to capture information that may be very "function specific."

As is the case with the information you are collecting, the benchmarking network should be considered a dynamic resource, not a static one. Just as your benchmarking information requirements change over time and by project, so too will your benchmarking network evolve over time. As you gain more benchmarking experience, your information network will become more diverse, involving more people and reference resources.

The objective is to develop a benchmarking information network that works for you. As you gain experience with benchmarking, the amount of time and effort needed to find the information you need will decrease, and the process of collecting benchmarking information will become easier. However, it requires a special effort to get your benchmarking information network established, and in some cases, this means a significant amount of time and frustration. There is a natural temptation to take information shortcuts when you first start out. Relying on the familiar or the friendly, or believing that you just don't have the time or the need to engage in serious investigational methods, is a real threat to the quality of your benchmarking information. Taking shortcuts early in the benchmarking process is one of the warning signs of process breakdown and lack of process discipline.

Identifying Information Resources

You are not the only one who has a need for comparative information. The more you investigate, the more you will discover that you are not alone. Everyone is after the same thing you are—quality information about somebody else.

1. *Where are the valid and reliable sources of benchmarking information?* Information is everywhere, whether you are seeking it out or whether it is thrust upon you during the normal course of business (or life). One point is clear: There definitely is no shortage of information. The challenge for benchmarkers is finding that set of information which is directly relevant to the subject being benchmarked and which can be counted on as valid and reliable.

What is valid information? *Validity* has to do with the integrity and "soundness" of a piece of information. First of all, is the information correct? Does it accurately reflect the subject or object it is meant to describe? Are the sources of information known for representing information accurately and honestly? If a resource nominates an organization as representing best practices in the area you are investigating, how certain are you that the reference has value? In general, the more you trust the source of a referral or piece of information, the more likely you will consider it valid and therefore place a higher value on it. For example, if you read about an organization in *The Wall Street Journal*, would you place a higher value on that information than on the same information heard from a stranger while riding the subway? Which piece of information would you be more likely to repeat to your coworkers as representing fact? Which source would you consider the most trustworthy and factual? Hopefully, it would be the internationally recognized business newspaper.

One of the challenges for new benchmarkers is building up an "inventory" of valid information sources—sources that can be trusted to produce benchmarking leads that can add value to your information search. Valid sources tend to be licensed or accredited (e.g., universities), official (e.g., government agencies), expert (e.g., analysts, consultants), and formal (e.g., business and trade journals). Too often, the inexperienced benchmarker will place too much confidence in word-of-mouth, second-hand references, or unpublished reports—sources that represent fairly low levels of validity. At the very least, you should attempt to avoid them. At best, you should attempt to create a benchmarking index of sources with a proven record for producing useful and factual information. The information resources described in this chapter represent a broad variety of organizations, individuals, institutions, associations, and publications that have demonstrated their long-term validity.

What is reliable information? Like validity, *reliability* has a lot to do with the trustworthiness of a source. Researchers and benchmarkers also use the term to describe the consistency of information over time. For example, if I ask a factual question of an official subject matter expert (e.g., a noted author) and record the response accurately, I should be fairly confident that if I were to return to the same individual in three months and pose the same question, I would receive a nearly identical answer. In other words, the information is reliable if it can be reported factually regardless of the time, day, or week in which the information was collected. You want to feel confident that a question asked at two different times will elicit the same response (provided the facts haven't changed over time). Again, the information resources described in this chapter have established a reputation for reliability.

2. *Which sources of benchmarking information are accessible to me?* Information won't be of much use if you don't have access to it. It is one

thing to identify valid and reliable sources of information; it is another to have access to these sources and get a satisfactory response from them. One of the difficulties of benchmarking is securing "quality time" from the information resources you have identified. Even getting others to return your introductory calls can be extremely frustrating. The value of establishing your own benchmarking information network over time is evident simply from the amount of time you will save just by getting a more timely response to your initial telephone contacts.

The resources presented on the following pages have been recommended by experienced researchers and benchmarkers, partly because they are accessible and familiar with basic research processes and methods. When approached, these sources were found to be responsive in helping organizations fulfill their information requirements.

You will quickly discover that there are many more sources of information than you had imagined. The challenge is to identify benchmark partners that will provide you with useful information in your quest for best practices and continuous improvement.

The Search for Best Practices

One of the common themes of benchmarking, as reflected in the definition menu presented in Chapter 1, is a search for industry or functional activities or outputs that can be classified as best-in-class, as world-class, or as representing best practices. The basic premise of benchmarking is to learn something of value from someone or someplace else, something that helps you perform more effectively or efficiently. The goal of most benchmarking activities is to learn from the best. Why set your sights on the middle when you can shoot for the top? This premise makes a lot of sense, and it is probably the most frequently cited reason for engaging in the benchmarking process.

How does one go about discovering what best practices or best-in-class really is? The answer that everyone wants to hear is to look in the "Benchmarking Directory"—you know, the one that lists best-practices companies by functional area and industry. This used to be a joke, but the fact is that today there are companies and associations that claim to offer just that. They have conducted their own investigations and identified the best-practices companies for you. All you have to do is ask for the information. The price varies, but be assured that most of these companies are profit-oriented, and the information you want may be very closely linked to the consulting services they want to sell. The important point to remember is that these companies represent only a single source of best-practices information. Their recommendations and referrals should be combined with other sources of information to define best practices for your particular area of interest.

Let's examine the types of sources that are used by experienced benchmarking companies to locate best-practices companies.

Best-in-Class or Best-in-Cleveland?

Many companies that claim to investigate best-in-class or best practices do only a superficial job of identifying and selecting benchmark partners. The following is a typical scenario.

A group of people decides to benchmark a particular subject. Members' level of expertise on the subject is extensive; in fact, they are the content experts on the subject for their particular organization. Once they have defined the subjects of their benchmarking investigation (or CSFs), they identify those organizations that represent best-in-class or best practices. In many cases, this identification process consists of a brainstorming session in which members of the group identify companies that, in their experience, represent best practices. This type of brainstorming may produce a list of twenty or more organizations covering a wide variety of companies both within and outside the industry group. The group then proceeds to develop a plan to contact these companies or, if the list is too long, the group narrows the list down to a more manageable size. In essence, this initial list of companies becomes *the* list of organizations that will be benchmarked. In some cases, a few other companies may be added or deleted. However, the assumption is that this initial list represents the core of the best-practices organizations to be investigated.

Does this scenario sound OK to you? What are the potential disadvantages of this approach? To answer this question, think about the manager who drew the series of boxes that represented levels of exposure to information and ideas (see Exhibit 1-4 in Chapter 1). The inner box represented his own department, the box that surrounded it represented the competition, the third box represented the industry group, and the fourth and fifth boxes represented business practices in any organization. The message was to encourage people to think "out of the box" when using the benchmarking process—to broaden their exposure to new ideas and methods. The process of identifying best practices also requires some thinking outside of the box that is defined by your own personal experience or exposure. Let's go back to the group that was described in the example. Their brainstorming exercise may not represent a thorough cross section of best-practices organizations. Their list of companies is affected by the level of experience and exposure of the team members. If their personal backgrounds, work experiences, tenure, educational levels, and professional networking activities (among other variables) are similar, then their list of best-practices companies may actually represent a narrow perspective.

The situation just described is not uncommon. For many organizations, this type of process for identifying best-practices organizations is typical. I call this type of process "best-in-Cleveland," based on an experience I had in a benchmarking seminar held in the Midwest. Some novice benchmarkers from Cleveland were participating in a small-group exercise in which they were asked to develop a strategy to identify best-practices companies in their functional area (shipping and receiving). They produced a list of fourteen best-practices companies. When asked to describe their strategy for selecting those fourteen companies, they identified one of their three selection criteria as "not more than a two-hour drive from Cleveland." Although it is possible that a few of these companies truly represent best shipping and receiving practices, it is more likely that the group merely identified best shipping and receiving practices within a two-hour drive of Cleveland. Limited information resources produce information of limited value.

Best-in-Class, World-Class, or Best Practices?

Some of the common terminology used in benchmarking has to do with the selection of benchmark partners that represent the desired state of organizational performance. In the benchmarking menu (see Exhibit 1-1 in Chapter 1), the terms used to describe these partner companies include *best-in-class, world-class,* and *best practices.* Do these terms really mean the same thing? I often ask companies to define what they expect in terms of comparative information when they conduct a benchmarking investigation. What I am really asking for is a statement of their realistic objectives. Their responses to this question include everything from "an improvement over our current practices" to "true world leadership."

Exhibit 5-2. The search for best practices.

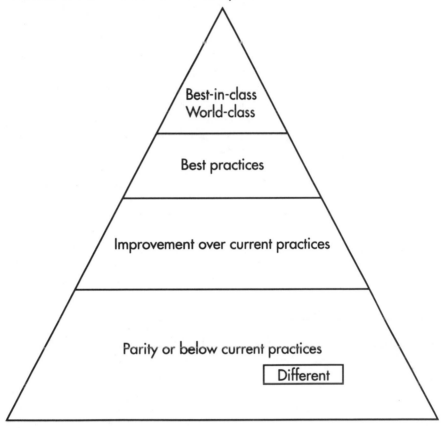

Exhibit 5-2 is a pyramid-shaped diagram that can be used to demonstrate the relative amounts of information that are available for consideration, depending on how an organization defines its benchmarking and improvement objectives. At the very top of the pyramid are the best-in-class and world-class practices, followed by a larger area representing best practices and an even larger area representing improvement over current practices. Note that the opportunities for simple improvement are much greater than the opportunities defined by the best-practices or best-in-class category. As an organization attempts to identify and analyze business practices at the top of the pyramid, the amount of resources required (e.g., time, funds, people) to pinpoint specific organizations and their activities also increases.

I always find it interesting and important to ask prospective bench-markers what they really want to gain from the process. After considering the pyramid as shown in Exhibit 5-2, it is amazing how many people admit that they would truly be content with basic improvement over current practices. In fact, after gaining some exposure to true "best practices" information, many organizations rethink their benchmarking objectives and quickly shift their direction lower down the pyramid to a more realistic or "comfortable" position.

A note of caution: If your benchmarking objective is to investigate best practices, exercise caution as you evaluate potential benchmark partners and the information you collect from them. Do your bench-mark partners really represent best practices, or do they simply offer you an alternative to your current business practices and represent something that is simply "different?" If you do not exercise caution or invest sufficient time in the process of selecting partners and evaluating information, you may think that you have moved "up the pyramid" toward best practices, while in fact you have not even identified a legitimate improvement opportunity. As you can see in Exhibit 5-2, one must be careful not to ascribe "improvement" to a product or process that is, in reality, merely "different." This problem is often encountered when benchmarkers are under pressure to produce benchmarking infor-mation, particularly under a tight deadline. People in this situation will often take process shortcuts and fail to "validate" their sources or the information that is provided to them. When pressed to make a recom-mendation or produce information, some benchmarkers will base their recommendations on whatever information they can get their hands on, whether that information represents a valid improvement opportunity or not.

Companies that are simply trying to identify improvement oppor-tunities generally limit their searches to companies from which they can learn something new that can be of benefit. This type of strategy may actually support the best-in-Cleveland approach mentioned earlier. At the other extreme, companies seeking true world-class benchmarks often make extensive use of databases, international networks and associations, and international consulting firms to locate true world-class performers.

Every organization that decides to embark on the benchmarking path should consider the fundamental issue of its goals and objectives. For most organizations, the goal of continuous improvement in a learning environment is challenging enough. Certainly benchmarking provides sufficient stimulation and information to help any organization achieve this objective. However, to become best-in-class or world-class represents a tremendous leap in ambition and implies a much more sophisticated view of information gathering and analysis—if not in content, at least in scope. Somewhere in between these extremes is the search for best practices. For most organizations, this is an ambitious undertaking. It requires a dedication to search beyond the new and improved to identify outputs and processes that really set the standard. Organizations should consider their benchmarking objectives carefully. A realistic definition of one's true objectives backed by a realistic commitment of resources is of greater value than setting a lofty goal and managing to reach only the middle of the pyramid.

Reliable Sources of Best Practices: Seeking Convergence

What are the most reliable sources for identifying best practices? Although the answer to this question does not encourage those looking for an easy answer, it does indicate a consistent and reliable approach that can be adopted by any type of organization. Experienced benchmarkers all mention certain general categories of references that should be checked as sources of best-practices information.

The process of identifying best-practices companies is usually as follows: The benchmarking team identifies the specific CSFs or functional areas to be benchmarked. A set of resources is identified for investigation (described later). The members of the benchmarking team engage in a basic search of these information sources and meet to compare notes on the organizations identified in their search. As the team examines the companies that emerge from this round of investigation, they are looking for convergence in the names that are mentioned—some level of agreement among the sources checked regarding the best-practices companies. These companies become preferred subjects for further investigation.

The six most commonly mentioned sources of information for identifying best-practices companies are listed here. They are not listed in any particular order of importance or preference, and the use of these different sources will vary by organization. A key point to remember, however, is that experienced benchmarking companies attempt to check as many of these sources as possible to seek some level of convergence of opinion. The more sources checked and the greater agreement among them, the greater the chance that the companies identified truly represent best practices.

1. *Special awards/citations*. Organizations that are formally recognized for product or service excellence by credible independent sources, such as the Malcolm Baldrige National Quality Award and the Deming Prize, are likely best-practices candidates. Specific awards presented by industry groups, trade associations, professional associations, and other official groups are easy to track by functional area. Awards or citations bestowed by special-interest publications, newspapers, or professional journals also identify specific achievements by functional area. Although these types of awards may have little to do with the overall bottom-line performance of organizations, they do highlight specific areas of excellence that provide leads for functional best practices.

2. *Media attention*. Organizations that are frequently cited in the media, especially the popular press and the business press, often gain a reputation for being exemplary. For example, Nordstrom Department Stores, McDonald's, and British Airways are frequently cited in the popular press for their customer-service policies and practices. Over time, these companies have become almost synonymous with the subject of customer service. Magazines such as *Fortune* regularly publish feature articles, such as "America's Most Admired Corporations," that rank companies by industry group according to a set of fairly generic criteria (e.g., product quality, customer service, corporate responsibility). These types of articles printed in mass-circulation periodicals tend to reinforce the excellent image of many well-established companies. Large-scale searches of media information can be done with relative ease by making use of the dozens of on-line databases that are available in most libraries and research departments.

3. *Professional associations*. Professional associations and societies are often able to provide recommendations regarding best practices by functional area. Virtually every professional function is represented by at least several reliable formal associations with extensive memberships. The membership lists of these professional groups include every type of organization—large and small, public and private, foreign and domestic. In most cases, these associations provide excellent referrals whether you and your organization are members of the association or not. Larger

associations maintain extensive functional databases and reference libraries, most of which are accessible without cost or for a nominal fee. Professional associations also sponsor national and regional conferences, symposia, and conventions. These meetings and their recorded minutes and proceedings provide valuable information regarding state-of-the-art developments.

4. *Independent reports.* Special reports prepared by trade and professional organizations, consumer organizations, analysts, government agencies, specialized institutes, or universities all tend to draw attention to organizations that are identified as being special or exemplary. These reports are often widely circulated among functional professionals, usually on demand. They are also available to the public, although one must usually be on some type of mailing list to keep informed of the availability of new reports or studies. Independent reports are often viewed as reliable, unbiased sources of information.

5. *Word of mouth.* In many cases, organizational reputations are enhanced by professionals who speak positively about an organization to other professionals. Positive comments from a respected and trusted professional tend to be repeated to others. This type of reinforcement creates an impression among large groups of professionals in a relatively short time. Professional conferences, conventions, seminars, and workshops are excellent opportunities for specialists to gauge the state of the art in their specialty areas. Formal and informal networks of functional specialists are often excellent sources of references for best-practices companies, particularly when these networks are supported by resources such as newsletters, on-line databases, and regional meetings. Each member of a benchmarking team brings his or her own personal professional network to the table when the team is identifying best-practices companies.

6. *Consultants.* Consultants often specialize in providing state-of-the-art information regarding specific functional areas. Reputable consulting companies, both large and small, are beginning to specialize in benchmarking services that include the identification of best-practices companies and the ability to introduce companies to one another as members of benchmarking consortia. However, caution should be exercised when using special benchmarking services, such as lists of best practices by functional area. These lists are only a single source of information and should be considered in conjunction with other sources.

Beware of the "Halo Effect"

When selecting benchmark partners, exercise caution not to fall victim to the halo effect. *Halo effect* is a psychological term that describes a characteristic defect in rating scales: to rate individuals either too high or too low on the basis of one outstanding trait. In plain English, it can be described as painting with too broad a brush. For example, individuals who are extremely intelligent are often ascribed other traits, such as being quiet or reserved. I have found two types of halo effects that are typical among benchmarking teams, even among experienced benchmarkers. I call these effects halo positive and halo negative. Avoid both types of effects as you conduct your search for benchmark partners.

Halo Positive

The halo postive effect occurs when an organization establishes a reputation for doing one thing particularly well. As a result, many assume that the company does other things or most things well. For example, companies that have won the Malcolm Baldrige National Quality Award report that they are overwhelmed with requests for site visits and interviews from companies benchmarking (or simply measuring) everything from accounting practices to physical facility designs. A woman who attended a benchmarking seminar kept naming IBM as a company that she wanted to investigate (her area of responsibility was human resources) regardless of the topic being discussed. I asked her why she mentioned IBM all the time and she replied, "I just love Baldrige winners!" (A Baldrige groupie?) People assume that because a company has won a major quality award, it is a natural candidate for investigation in any functional area, whether or not it has an established reputation in that area. I call this effect halo positive because of the tendency to assume that a company's reputation for excellence in a single functional area or activity correlates highly with excellence in other areas as well. Although there is often much truth to this line of thinking, it should not be considered a given.

Halo Negative

The halo negative effect is evident when considering companies whose overall performance or recent market history indicates a significant organizational depression or downturn. Because the organization is in a slump, it is often overlooked as a resource for any type of benchmarking, even though some functional activities may represent best practices. People who have a superficial understanding of the benchmarking process may question the benchmarking of companies whose overall performance levels are down. An explanation of functional benchmarking and the investigation of specific CSFs should overcome this tendency toward halo-negative thinking.

Seeking Cooperative Benchmark Partners

Perhaps the biggest hurdle people have to contend with as they become familiar with the process of benchmarking is the psychological barrier against calling on individuals in other organizations—particularly competitors. For most people, fraternizing with the competition is not a normal activity, and this preexisting notion may be used to defend a position against using the benchmarking process.

People may attempt to find excuses for not benchmarking, such as claiming that all data are sensitive or proprietary. Some may project their own fears onto benchmark partners and assume that other organizations would not cooperate in a benchmarking investigation (asking the what's-in-it-for-me? question on behalf of the other organizations). People from small and medium-size companies wonder why large Fortune 500–type companies would cooperate with them. They are apprehensive about how they will present themselves to larger, better-known companies. Others immediately claim that there are possible antitrust implications without ever exploring the issue with qualified legal counsel. All of these "defense mechanisms" are common among people who, for whatever reason, do not want to participate in the benchmarking process or who are apprehensive about the unknown.

Why do employees feel uncomfortable about direct contact with employees from other organizations? I can think of three reasons:

1. *Tradition*. The stereotype of the competitor as the bad guy and the enemy dies hard.

2. *Collusion*. Many people fear that making direct contact with competitors' employees and possibly sharing information with them is a form of collusion. In some industries (e.g., the oil industry) there are

indeed historical precedents regarding certain forms of information sharing. The fact is that most of the information shared could not be interpreted as collusion—either legally or professionally—as long as good judgment and a bit of caution are properly exercised.

3. *Awkwardness*. Quite simply, many people feel awkward calling on employees from other organizations—particularly competitors. This feeling is often extinguished after some experience breaking the ice.

The good news about this initial reluctance is that once the actual attempt is made to gather benchmarking information through direct contact with people in other organizations, novice benchmarkers are often pleasantly surprised (and in many cases shocked) at the relative ease of collecting information in this manner. In fact, many people are surprised at the level of curiosity and cooperation they receive, even from employees of competing companies. For most people, it has to be experienced to be believed.

At some point, almost everyone who benchmarks is asked why people from other companies—especially competitors—cooperate in the data-collection effort at all. There are several answers:

1. *Professional affiliation*. Many benchmarking contacts with other organizations, including competitors, are made by one functional professional to another (e.g., one engineering manager to another). There is usually a certain degree of familiarity and professionalism established immediately. Benchmarking employees often share similar professional experiences and career histories with their counterparts in other organizations. Many professionals who participate in this level of communication share affiliations in professional organizations, networks, and societies. Many of them know the same people through these networks and some have actually met at conferences or conventions. Once this level of connection is made, the process of information exchange is greatly enhanced.

2. *Curiosity*. The process of communicating on this level is by its nature interesting. There is a natural curiosity about what other organizations are doing, and this level of contact provides an opportunity to satisfy one's curiosity regarding life on the other side. Just the mention of the word *benchmarking* to a potential benchmark partner creates interest among those who are curious about the process and provides a break in the everyday business routine.

3. *The opportunity to learn something.* There is certainly an element of personal and professional learning that can take place as part of the benchmarking process. The opportunity to learn something new or to confirm long-held beliefs about one's own or someone else's business practices is an attractive and powerful inducement for participation and cooperation. An IBM benchmarker said that his organization classifies benchmarking in almost the same category as training—both activities represent opportunities for personal development and learning.

4. *Reciprocity.* There is an element of give-and-take in the process of collecting benchmarking information. Employees from other organizations often agree to participate in a benchmarking investigation if they believe they can receive something in return, such as a copy of the benchmarking report being generated. In many situations, benchmark partners express an interest in a different subject and agree to cooperate with the understanding that reciprocity will occur at a later time. In other cases there is no expectation of reciprocity at all. Often the offer to share information regarding the work you are doing—even a summary report—is enough to gain the cooperation of benchmark partners.

5. *Courtesy.* Many people cooperate with data-collection efforts out of a sense of personal or professional courtesy. If the request for benchmarking information is handled in a professional manner, and if some type of formal documentation accompanies the request, most companies will cooperate within reason.

In summary, the person-to-person benchmarking connection is the source of much debate and speculation among people who have never participated in a formal benchmarking project. However, people with experience in the benchmarking process soon develop an awareness of the potential reactions and a realistic expectation of how their requests for information will be received. One of the more difficult challenges of the benchmarking process is to begin the first project—to overcome the rationalization, the fear, and the excuses. In some organizations, pilot benchmarking projects are initiated as a way to test the waters and demonstrate that the process is feasible in a particular organization's environment.

Benchmarking Networks: A Core Group of Benchmark Partners

One of the most recent phenomena in the practice of benchmarking involves the formation of formal benchmarking networks or consortia.

These groups band together for the explicit purpose of opening bench-marking channels among the participating members. As members of these networks begin the benchmarking process, their fellow network members represent an automatic starting point for identifying potential benchmark partners. Even if the network members are not included as benchmark partners for a particular investigation, they do represent another valuable resource that can be checked to find potential candi-dates for benchmarking. Also, members of these networks may agree to share information from benchmarking reports that have already been completed.

Some of these benchmarking networks are formed by organizations that are members of a particular industry group. For example, a group of eighteen corporations in the telecommunications industry (e.g., AT&T, Bell Atlantic, NYNEX, MCI, GTE) banded together to form the Telecommunications Benchmarking Consortium. This group was formed to stimulate benchmarking activities in a variety of generic areas (e.g., maintenance, customer satisfaction, new-product development, service), not just on subjects specific to their industry group. Other networks consist of functional specialists from a variety of organizations representing different industries. An example of a functional network is a group called the Financial Quality Network, comprising specialists primarily from the financial departments of companies such as Federal Express, Caterpillar, Xerox, Westinghouse, DEC, and Du Pont. This particular network expressed a desire to create an open-door policy on benchmarking. Even though this group consists predominantly of finan-cial specialists, it recognized the value of creating a network that would encourage benchmarking in virtually any functional area. Other func-tional benchmarking networks have been formed in areas such as engineering, manufacturing, and human resources.

These kinds of benchmarking networks have proved to be an effective means of initiating benchmarking investigations and taking advantage of the benchmarking resources of a large number of cooper-ative organizations. Many of the companies that are asked to participate in these networks have already established a reputation for their use of the benchmarking process. They do not have to be convinced of the merits of benchmarking, and they already understand the value of participating in joint benchmarking ventures.

Informal networking opportunities are being stimulated by the growth of benchmarking conferences and symposia sponsored by inde-pendent research groups and associations. These conferences are held regionally and are usually well attended by people who are looking for benchmarking opportunities in their functional areas or their industry groups. Many ad hoc networks are formed at these types of meetings, which are becoming more frequent and better organized.

Other Sources of Benchmarking Information

Up until this point, we have discussed benchmark partners as including organizations or their employees. These are the direct sources of benchmarking information that provide you with best-practices examples and other comparative data. However, there are other useful sources that can help you locate best-practices companies and other information pertinent to your investigation. This section briefly describes the kinds of resources that benchmarking companies have found useful as they begin a benchmarking analysis. These resources can be used by any benchmarking company, regardless of industry, size, location, or ownership.

Although the process of benchmarking is just beginning to reach maturity in some organizations, the process of collecting business information has a relatively long history in most companies. Many of the sources of reliable benchmarking information are identical to the sources that have been used to research new technologies, analyze market conditions, and investigate competitive practices.

Organizations that collect benchmarking information generally focus their data-collection activities around a common core of information sources. A question posed to the best-practices benchmarking companies was, "Where do you find valid and reliable resources to help you identify and contact potential benchmarking partners?" The numerous sources mentioned tended to cluster into seven key categories:

1. *Government sources*—federal, state, and local resources
2. *Subject matter experts*—including consultants, academics, and analysts
3. *Special-interest groups*—trade and professional associations or networks
4. *The media*—trade and professional publications and journals, general business-related publications, and government-generated materials

5. *Employees, customers, and suppliers*—those most familiar with your organization and it's processes
6. *Benchmark partners*—referrals from best-practices organizations (i.e., whom *they* benchmark)
7. *Foreign data sources*—banks, multi-national corporate offices, foreign consulates, international databases

Each of these benchmarking information sources is reviewed here, including specific examples of organizations, associations, publications, indexes, databases, and agencies recommended by experienced benchmarkers. These references should help you build your own internal benchmarking intelligence library. (Exhibit 5-3 provides a summary table of the resources listed in this chapter.)

Government Sources

Government sources, particularly federal agencies, have been particularly helpful to benchmarkers, primarily with respect to the written publications that the government develops, collects, catalogs, and makes available to the general public. While much of the information is too broad to address the specific information needs of most benchmarking efforts, government reports, directories, and experts have generally proved to be excellent leads when investigating best-practices candidates. To the surprise of many benchmarkers who have not had any previous direct dealings with government agencies, government employees are generally extremely helpful and knowledgeable when it comes to tracking down specific information. Most benchmarkers report success at locating useful information after only a few calls to the appropriate government agency. Another frequently cited benefit of working with government sources is that they are relatively inexpensive, and in many cases there are no expenditures at all except for the time required to make the appropriate calls. However, much of the information collected by the federal government is not timely—for example, some information collected on an annual basis may not reflect more recent events or developments.

Federal Government

Most federal agencies have established liberal policies about sharing information with individuals who have specific information needs. If these agencies do not have the specific information you seek, they can often assist you in locating source directories, publication indexes, and leads to professional associations, other government agencies, and subject matter experts.

With respect to general business information about specific organizations, the federal government oversees the development of regulations, standards, and guidelines with respect to a variety of documents that are required to be produced by publicly held organizations. It also supports several organizations that collect, analyze, and store vast amounts of information about specific businesses and industries. A review of some of the major government sources of information should include the following:

- *"Washington Information Directory."* This document is an excellent guide to information sources, both federal and private, that reside in the Washington, D.C., area. The Directory provides a good overview of the various specialty divisions contained within the larger government agencies. Names and telephone numbers of key contacts in these organizations are also provided. The Directory is published by the *Congressional Quarterly*, and is available in most major research libraries.

- *Annual reports.* The typical annual report is a good starting place for investigating another organization. It contains all sorts of valuable information, starting with the overall balance sheet, which usually reflects the organization's financial performance for the previous three to five years, usually described in some form of narrative within the body of the report. Other types of information covered by an annual report include reviews of new products; descriptions of new business ventures; statements about corporate mission, vision, and values; staffing charts; messages from senior management; statements concerning pending litigation; and general articles about diverse subjects such as employees, customers, new technologies, new products, and general strategic directions. Copies of annual reports are usually distributed free of charge by the organizations themselves and can generally be obtained through the office of the corporate secretary or public relations department. The U.S. Securities and Exchange Commission (SEC) is responsible for maintaining files of annual reports. Contact the SEC at 1100 L Street NW, Washington, DC 20549.

(text continues on page 128)

Exhibit 5-3. Sources of benchmarking information.

Government

Federal Government
       Agency experts
       Annual reports
       Federal contracts
       Federal publications
       10-Ks

■ State Government
       Business directories
       Legal documents

Subject Matter Experts

■ Academic Institutions
  Consultants
■ Investment Analysts

Trade and Professional Organizations and Networks

Conferences, Meeting
■ Membership Networks
  Research Support Services
■ Specialist Publications

Publications

Business Information Services
■ Market Research Studies
  On-Line Databases
  Private Business Presses
  Publication Indexes and Directories

Employees, Customers, Suppliers

- ■ Distributors
- ■ Internal Research Staff
- ■ Internal Subject Matter Experts
- ■ Manufacturers
- Retailers
- Suppliers

Benchmark Partners

- Benchmarking Databases
- Best-Practices Organizations
- ■ References, Introductions

Foreign Data Sources

- Banks
- Consulates
- Foreign Chambers of Commerce
- ■ Foreign Libraries
- International Trade Commission/Association
- ■ Securities Brokers
- Specialized Databases
- Trade Associations

■ *Form 10-K.* Filed annually, the 10-K is a detailed financial document that reviews an organization's financial statements for a period of five years. It includes such information as a balance sheet, sales (by category), debt levels, and depreciation schedules. It also includes information about competitors, organizational strategies, and structural changes—in short, any significant factor that may affect the price of the organization's stock. The Form 10-K can also be accessed via the SEC and from some private companies, who will forward it directly to you.

■ *Federal contract information.* Under the Freedom of Information Act (FOIA), you may be able to receive copies of contracts that organizations have established with the federal government. Besides the specifications of the contract, these documents can provide useful information about an organization's structure, performance capabilities, technologies, strategic direction, and production schedules. Requests for contract documentation are directed through the federal agency responsible for the contract. There is some variance in the policies and procedures of federal agencies, which may affect the cost of securing these documents (usually involving research and reproduction costs) as well as the amount of time required to respond to information requests. Contact the Freedom of Information Clearinghouse, Suite 700, 2000 P Street NW, P.O. Box 19367, Washington, DC 20036.

■ *"U.S. Industrial Outlook."* The Department of Commerce publishes this document annually. It focuses on an organization's shipment values over a five-year period, providing annual and long-term projections for hundreds of manufacturing and service-based industries. This document can be ordered from the Superintendent of Documents, U.S. Government Printing Office, Washington, DC 20402.

■ *National Technical Information Service (NTIS).* The NTIS is an excellent source of information about U.S.- and foreign-government–supported engineering and R&D activities. NTIS maintains records on a vast number of technical reports and publishes a weekly newsletter that provides abstracts of reports on file. NTIS makes available the results of "Published Searches," which are compilations of abstracts on specific subject areas, and also supports the Center for the Utilization of Federal Technology (CUFT). CUFT provides information about research developed at various federal research laboratories. It also publishes directories of government sources of R&D expertise and information about laboratories and research agencies engaged in state-of-the-art R&D activities. These resources have typically been very helpful to benchmarkers in terms of their frankness and cooperation in helping organizations identify federally supported research activities. Contact the NTIS through the U.S. Department of Commerce, Springfield, VA 22161.

■ *National Institute of Standards and Technology (NIST).* NIST has gained fame for benchmarkers as the government organization responsible for the development and administration of the Malcolm Baldrige National Quality Award. Beyond this distinction, NIST is an excellent resource for any investigation having to do with standards or measures, particularly in areas such as manufacturing, engineering, and computer science. It also publishes an excellent directory entitled "Cooperative Research Opportunities at NIST," which lists the names and locations of experts in the field of standards and measures. Contact the U.S. Department of Commerce, National Institute of Standards and Technology, Research Information Center, Gaithersburg, MD 20899.

State and Local Governments

There's a lot you can learn from state and local governments. For benchmarking purposes, the most useful sources of state-level information are usually connected with a state Department of Commerce or some other department dealing with business development. Each state varies with respect to the quality and quantity of information that it will provide to the public. Initial contacts with state agencies often begin simply by consulting the Blue Pages in the telephone directory under "State Government," which lists most major agencies and departments. The general information operator can connect you with the various individuals who can get you started when tracking down state information sources.

■ *"State Executive Directory."* This guide, which is usually found in most large public libraries, provides a useful index of the various agencies and offices in each state. The names, titles, and locations of specific state employees are included together with a general subject index. The *State Executive Directory* is published by the Carroll Publishing Company.

■ *State corporate filings.* Articles of incorporation, which describe details of business operations, structure, and general financial information, are often required to be filed with the state. A good place to begin the search for these types of documents is the Office of the State Secretary.

Subject Matter Experts

Subject matter experts are those individuals who are specifically trained, informed, and recognized as authorities with respect to the specific subject being benchmarked. While many claim to be experts in their fields, the quest for best-practices information should include a search for those who have established a consistent and formally recognized status as valid sources of functional information. Subject matter experts may include academics, consultants, and analysts who specialize in the area you are benchmarking. While many, if not most, subject matter experts earn their livings by researching and sharing information, they are often willing to provide benchmarkers with excellent leads to best-practices organizations without imposing a fee for their services (within reasonable bounds, of course).

Academic Institutions

Academics conduct important research in almost every endeavor that affects the world of business. These researchers may provide useful input such as publications, special detailed studies, and access to research centers for collecting important historical data.

Many colleges and universities have a public relations office that will refer you to the appropriate department. Most departmental staffs can direct you to a faculty member who can answer your questions. Some academic institutions maintain databases that list faculty members and other authorities by their areas of expertise. The institution's public relations office can tell you if that type of database is available.

■ *Academic libraries.* Many academic libraries are open to the public. Most large academic libraries provide facilities that for a fee, can perform computerized database searches for your organization. To find an academic library in your area, contact the Association of College and Research Libraries, American Library Association, 50 Huron Street, Chicago, IL 60611. The Association provides free help in finding college and research libraries that specialize in your subject of interest.

Consultants

Consultants can include all types of specialists, expert witnesses, and security analysts. Consultants find their own niches, particularly in the technical fields. Directories may help you find specialized consultants to help you with your data search. The advantage of consultants is that many of them are outstanding experts in their field and can provide a great deal of inside information, advice, and in-depth knowledge. The role of consultants who specialize in providing benchmarking services was reviewed in Chapter 4. Benchmarking consultants cover a range of activities from benchmarking training to process consultation to total process and project management. For some organizations, consultants provide a valuable resource and enable the benchmarking process to succeed, particularly when the organization's internal expertise or personnel availability is scarce. However, caution should be exercised when making use of consultants so that the organization does not become dependent on the consultant's services at the expense of developing its own internal expertise. And organizations should always conduct a reference check prior to contracting any benchmarking responsibilities to an outside consultant.

■ *"Consultants and Consulting Organizations Directory"* (*Gale Research*). This directory lists thousands of consultants in over 150 fields.

Investment Analysts

Investment analysts usually specialize in a focused subject area and often have access to strategic and marketing-related information that may not be publicly available. Organizations often plan much of their new product and strategic announcements specifically for the analyst audience, hoping to receive favorable reviews when the analysts publish their reports on particular organizations or industries. Their reports can often be accessed directly through the analysts themselves or through their firms, and are often provided free or for a nominal charge. In addition, organizations will often make available copies of analyst's reports that have been produced about them, particularly when the reports are favorable. Some on-line databases list sources of analysts reports or provide report summaries for a nominal fee.

■ *"Nelson's Directory of Investment Research."* This directory provides the names and addresses and areas of expertise of thousands of investment analysts. Contact W. R. Nelson & Company, 1 Gateway Plaza, Port Chester, NY 10573.

Trade and Professional Organizations and Networks

Perhaps the most accessible and user-friendly sources of benchmarking contacts are the professional organizations and networks. These organizations bring together individuals who often have similar backgrounds and share common interests. Membership in a professional organization, whether international, national, or local, permits access to member information resources and member directories. Membership in organizations and societies has proved to be a tremendous asset to new benchmarkers: It gives them a starting point, a reason for making contact, and an opportunity to communicate.

These organizations offer two distinct opportunities. First, if the professional network is extremely large, members of best-practices organizations might also be part of that network. This common link may greatly reduce the time it takes to develop a relationship with a prospective benchmark partner. The fact is that benchmarking relationships are most frequently established between individuals or small groups; rarely is the nature of the typical relationship a corporate-to-corporate affair. Individuals who share a common link may establish an informal relationship very quickly and without a tremendous amount of formal corporate posturing. The second advantage is that other members of the professional network may have leads to best-practices organizations (and be willing to share those leads), even if they themselves have not reached best-practices status. Perhaps they have even conducted a formal benchmarking investigation and would be willing to share some of their findings with you.

Professional organizations also offer advantages if they maintain professional libraries or research centers. Often these facilities represent comprehensive information databases that offer a variety of research support services to network members. In many cases, membership in the professional organization is not even required in order to gain access to its research resources (although nominal fees might be charged for access to information). Many professional organizations maintain extensive files on their member organizations and a working knowledge of key functional contacts. They may also employ staff specialists who work as research staff or in member relations. The more experienced employees of these organizations can often help you track down both organizational and individual contacts.

■ *"Encyclopedia of Associations" (Gale Research)*. This reference can be found in most libraries and contains the names and locations of over 15,000 associations and professional societies.

■ *"World Guide to Trade Organizations" (R. R. Bowker)*. A useful directory for locating the names and addresses of international trade associations. It is organized by country.

Publications

In addition to the printed materials produced by the information sources already mentioned, there are a tremendous number and variety of publications that cover virtually any subject that can be benchmarked. These publications are generally produced by the private business press (e.g., books, periodicals, and newspapers), information services companies (e.g., Standard & Poor's), and market research organizations. New benchmarkers are often shocked (and sometimes overwhelmed) by the number of publications and amount of information available with respect to their particular areas of interest. One engineering manager interested in researching technical training for electrical engineers was surprised to learn that there were over twenty-seven specific periodicals that dealt with this subject—and these were just U.S.-based publications! So if you haven't done much basic research since you've left school, be prepared for a surprise as you begin to investigate printed sources of best-practices activities.

Locating publications is not very difficult, although it may be time-consuming as you begin to identify the sources of most value to you. Naturally, publications will vary in format, length, frequency of publication, accessibility, and professionalism. However, your main concern should be with the value of the content. A fairly esoteric professional newsletter with a small distribution may be more valuable than a major business periodical targeted to your functional area of specialization. Experienced benchmarkers recommend that those who are starting out invest a sufficient amount of time during their early benchmarking investigations to become familiar with the wide variety of publications available to them.

Publication Indexes and Directories

Before you can review the information in a publication, you must first *locate* it. While the names and sources of well-known publications may not be difficult to find, small, esoteric, or foreign publications can take more effort to locate. Many excellent indexes and directories have proved to be extremely valuable to benchmarkers. Most of these can be found in major libraries, or even in the research libraries of many large organizations.

■ *"Business Periodicals Index" (H. W. Wilson Company).* This is an index to over 250 business periodicals covering a wide range of subject areas. Monthly supplements provide up-to-date information regarding new sources of information.

■ *"Standard Periodical Dictionary" (Oxbridge Communications).* This is a very thorough directory of periodicals, which includes many esoteric and hard-to-find publications.

■ *"The IMS Ayer Directory of Publications" (IMS Press).* This directory lists publications from the United States and Canada and includes a wide array of business publications. Names of editors are included.

■ *"Magazines for Libraries" (R. R. Bowker Company).* This directory references over 5,000 better-known publications that are considered to be the best in their fields. It provides a good review of the types of articles commonly found in each publication.

■ *"Willings Press Guide" (Thomas Skinner Directories).* This directory lists newspapers and periodicals by subject and by country—a good starting point for international periodical searches.

On-Line Databases

Since the early 1980s, there has been a tremendous surge in the number of on-line databases available to the general public (one estimate is that there are currently over 4,000 in existence). These databases summarize, index, and store vast amounts of information that can be accessed by keying in on specific words that define subject areas, authors, dates, and locations (e.g., countries). Once a set of key words has been identified, the computer searches through its records to locate articles, books, or references that contain the same key words. Obviously, a fairly specific set of key words is needed in order to prevent the database from producing hundreds, if not thousands, of references that have no connection to the specific subject you are investigating.

Databases can help you to find specific information regarding:

- Articles, periodicals, and books written on particular subjects
- Organizations associated with particular products, markets, or technologies
- Experts associated with particular subjects
- Associations and networks that attract members from certain industries and interests

Most major databases can be accessed by paying a fee to the company that owns and manages the database. Once you have subscribed to a database service, you may be able to access it directly through a personal computer via modem. If you are not planning to make extensive use of these databases, most large research libraries that subscribe to them will generate reports for you for a nominal fee. The database companies can frequently refer you to local database owners who will help you perform your search.

If you think a certain database holds promise, you may be able to get a good idea of its contents by referring to a database thesaurus. This type of publication also gives you information about using the database and may provide examples to help you to use it effectively.

Also worth knowing about are the update services that provide subscribers with regular reports noting changes in the databases. For example, Selective Dissemination of Information (SDI) allows database users to receive updates when changes are noted in specific types of information categories or when changes affect a particular organization's files.

■ *DIALOG.* This system represents one of the largest selections of databases for a variety of technical subject areas. Contact DIALOG Information Services, Inc., 3460 Hillview Avenue, Palo Alto, CA 94304.

■ *SDC/Orbit.* This system specializes in scientific and technical databases. Contact SDS, Santa Monica, CA.

■ *"Directory of Online Databases" (Cuadra/Elsevier).* This is actually a database directory that provides information about several thousand databases. It is updated quarterly.

Business Information Services

Business information services provide a wide variety of information about organizations, including information related to credit ratings, company history, structure, product and service information, and financial data. Although primarily used as credit reporting resources (e.g., Standard & Poor's, Dunn & Bradstreet), these services are valuable when tracking down basic information about an organization.

- *"Standard & Poor's Register of Corporations."* This is a frequently used general directory of company information. Volume 1 (entitled *Corporations*) is a useful starting place for beginning your information search. It lists basic information (e.g., addresses, names of key officers, subsidiaries, stock information, and basic financial data) for approximately 50,000 corporations.

- *"Moody's Manuals (Dunn & Bradstreet).* These manuals provide background and detail for a great number of companies, including information on history, products, structure, and financial information.

- *"Business Rankings" (Gale Research).* This directory ranks thousands of businesses by category according to performance. It has been cited as having some excellent utility as a starting point for tracking down best-practices candidates.

Market Research Studies

Market research studies are usually conducted by private organizations and institutions and generally cover specific topics such as the automobile or the oil industry. They are often available at a cost (which could be substantial) to anyone who can afford them. In some extreme cases, benchmarking organizations have actually commissioned market research studies to independently analyze competitor or industry trends. However, the cost of these reports makes such a practice rare in the world of benchmarking.

- *"Findex: The Directory of Market Research Reports, Studies, and Surveys" (National Standards Association). Findex* is a guide to commercially available market and business research. The Information Catalogue (FIND/SVP) is published every other month and includes reviews of market research studies in a variety of industry areas. Contact FIND/SVP, 625 Avenue of the Americas, New York, NY 10011.

Employees, Customers, and Suppliers

Some of the most accessible benchmarking information sources of best-practices competitive or industry organizations are employees, customers, and suppliers. These are the individuals and organizations with whom you have the most frequent and intense relationships. As information resources, they should be very accessible and will often provide you with useful information at very little, if any, cost and trouble. Particularly when benchmarking against competitors or within your own industry group against noncompetitors, customers and suppliers often provide you with invaluable insights concerning the business practices of your closest rivals. In many cases, these sources will take the time to provide you with information to promote their own causes as well—to challenge you to be a better supplier or customer yourself. In fact, in many cases you receive a tremendous amount of benchmarking-related information from these sources without asking for it— primarily due to the fact that these individuals and organizations tend to benefit when you make improvements in your organizational processes.

The possible downside of collecting information from these sources is that their perspectives are often biased too strongly toward their own self-interests. For example, customers will always want you to provide products and services that work better, are delivered faster, and cost less. Therefore, when requesting information about "best practices," you may receive information that leads to "best results" for the customer or supplier. The best antidote to this type of situation is to keep the benchmarking process as objective as possible from your end and to request that customers and suppliers substantiate their recommendations and referrals.

Your Own Organization

Employees in your own organization can provide you with very valuable information about other organizations.

■ *Strategic planning.* Employees responsible for strategic planning often act as de facto benchmarkers while performing their normal jobs. In many organizations, strategic planners maintain thorough files on the business practices of competitors and industry leaders. At the very least, strategic planners may provide excellent leads to subject matter experts and other sources who can help you perform your own specific benchmarking investigation.

■ *Purchasing, supplier contact personnel.* These employees can often provide valuable information regarding competitive pricing, quality levels, and distribution performance. They are also aware of imminent changes in pricing or product strategies, and can serve as effective barometers of competitors' reactions to a variety of market conditions.

■ *Engineering staff.* Engineering and design employees are often well aware of state-of-the-art design and development practices within your industry group. In some organizations, members of these departments are responsible for developing an intimate knowledge of competitive best practices by literally "dissecting" competitors' products and services through a variety of legal means. By maintaining memberships in professional organizations and societies, many engineers and designers also maintain a close professional watch on the state-of-the-art activities of organizations outside of your industry group.

■ *Marketing and service.* Your marketing and service employees often represent the "front line" to your customer base. They receive relevant and timely feedback from customers regarding their reactions to your products and services in relation to those offered by your competitors. Market research departments, such as strategic planning, often conduct formal analyses that are about as close as many organizations come to effective competitive benchmarking. Employees in these departments also represent a tremendous resource when they offer their expertise and services in the areas of database management and information analysis.

■ *Finance.* Many finance specialists can offer you valuable insight into the mangement practices of competitors, particularly when it is important to determine rates of investment in new technologies and processes. The finance staff can also provide a glimpse of reality when it comes to planning for future investments in the business. They often temper a search for best practices with the reality of what the organization can afford with respect to investment and change.

As discussed previously, the process of benchmarking often begins with a self-examination—internal benchmarking. In this situation, your employees and the organization itself (through its records) provide the information you need.

In addition, many organizations have in-house resources that are well equipped to help employees search for benchmarking-related information. These resources go by various names such as information resource centers, library services, and research centers. Although they are most commonly found in larger organizations that can afford to maintain a professional information research staff, these services are becoming more common in small and medium-size organizations that have extensive information needs.

Internal research facilities generally provide three basic services that support benchmarking activities. First, they maintain libraries of research publications like the ones mentioned in this chapter. They have the contacts and the experience necessary to acquire written materials and catalog them in a professional manner. Second, organization libraries and research centers can usually access databases. They are well equipped to run database searches or to work with the database companies and manage the search process. Third, in-house facilities can also assist benchmarkers in creating and maintaining benchmarking reporting systems, which include information such as benchmark partner profiles, site visit reports, benchmarking project summaries, and internal directories of benchmarking network members.

Benchmarking specialists at Caterpillar make use of their own business resource center to run searches for best-practices leads that might be contained in periodicals located on computer networks. They are able to search through the broad spectrum of business journals and periodicals as well as focus on specialized on-line databases. During initial benchmarking training sessions, new benchmarkers are introduced to this resource, made aware of key contacts at the center, and given guidance on proper and effective uses of the center's capabilities. Information requests are usually made using the team leader as a contact point. Du Pont also provides such instruction to its benchmarking facilitators during the training stage. The staff of its corporate business information services group routinely runs searches for benchmarking teams. At AT&T, the information resource center is staffed by library specialists who offer a variety of information-gathering and analysis services. Teams are encouraged to make use of these facilities during the orientation and training period.

If your organization has in-house research or library capabilities of the type just described, begin the process of establishing a benchmarking support capability with your professional research staff. Include information about such research capabilities as part of your formal benchmarking training or orientation sessions. Smaller organizations that don't have these types of internal research facilities can usually receive similar support services (e.g., database searches) from local college, university, or large public libraries. Certain consultants specialize in providing basic research and will collect and analyze information according to their clients' specifications.

Customers

Customers can be an excellent source of information regarding product preferences and service experiences. Organizations often use customers to provide feedback about their own products and services. However, in the process of benchmarking, customers are also used to provide information about the products and services offered by other organizations. For example, customers can be asked to describe which products and services meet their needs and why. They can give their perspective on excellent and poor customer-service practices. Customers can critique the products or services of your organization.

Customer information is often collected through surveys or focus groups. There is some concern about the honesty of this information. Since customers are often aware of the organization collecting the information, there is the possibility that they might somehow mask their true responses. One precautionary measure is to conceal your organization's sponsorship of the data-collection effort or to use consultants to perform the task of data collection.

Manufacturers and Suppliers

Manufacturers and suppliers can be very valuable in conducting competitive and industry benchmarking because they are likely to deal with other organizations whose processes or services are similar to yours. If the supplier is large and serves a diverse national or international client list, it may have some information that can steer you toward valuable benchmarking resources. However, local manufacturers and suppliers may have been exposed to the business practices of a limited number of organizations. While the information they offer may stimulate ideas for process or service improvements, it is risky to assume that this information represents competitive or industry best practices.

Manufacturers and suppliers are usually very cooperative in benchmarking investigations. However, they may be reluctant to provide information about your direct competitors unless your organization is participating in a study sponsored by a group of organizations that have agreed to share information. In these cases, manufacturers and suppliers should be briefed about the nature of the benchmarking agreement. They should also be shown some sort of formal document regarding the agreement among the project participants.

■ *"Thomas Register of American Manufacturers."* This comprehensive sixteen-volume directory lists the names of manufacturers in literally thousands of industries. It also provides brand or trade names, which can help you locate the manufacturer when you only know the name of the product or brand. The *Thomas Register* is carried by most major libraries.

Retailers and Distributors

If you sell your products through retailers, they can be an excellent source of information about organizations in your industry, and particularly about competitors. They can often provide detailed information about product marketing strategies and programs, pricing policies, special promotional activities, distribution practices, and product quality. Like manufacturers and suppliers, certain retailers may be reluctant to provide you with information about other organizations without the express consent of the other organization(s). It is recommended that you always comply with the protocol established by the specific retailer and not press for information considered to be confidential.

The key person in a retail environment is usually the buyer. Buyers maintain contact with a variety of individuals, including salespeople, other buyers, and distributors. They are often aware of the details of sales practices, pricing policies, and general marketing strategies of the organizations with whom they deal. They are also likely to know whom the benchmarker should contact in another organization.

■ *"Sheldon's Retail Stores"* (Phelon, Sheldon, and Marsar). An excellent general reference, this directory covers over 3,000 retail stores with emphasis on clothing, department, and home furnishings stores. Stores are arranged geographically, and there is an alphabetical index as well.

■ *"Stores of the World Directory"* (Newman Books). A good source for investigating international retailers, this reference lists all types of retailers, discounters, cooperatives, and buying groups.

Distributors are often excellent sources of information regarding the types and volumes of shipments being distributed by specific companies. Representatives of independent distributors often issue what are known as line cards. These describe the lines carried by the distributor, and include some specific details about the products themselves. Line cards can help you begin to understand the types and volume of products that are being distributed by another organization, and also where these goods are being shipped. You may be able to order copies of these line cards from distributors. Of course this information collection approach is more in line with traditional competitive analysis techniques, in that you are approaching a third party to find out about another organization, most likely a competitor. Exercise caution if you are collecting information from these types of sources while you are simultaneously attempting to collect information from competitors using more direct, face-to-face methods.

Benchmark Partners

If you have conducted a thorough search for best-practices benchmark partners and you believe that you have truly identified a set of best-practices organizations representing competitors, similar organizations, or functional/generic partners, then one of the more productive questions you can ask is whether *they* conduct any benchmarking analyses as they develop and improve their own products and services. The partner you have selected as a best-practices organization may have already conducted some level of formal investigation into the same (or very similar) processes as you have. If so, it may be able to share some of its information sources with you—or better yet, be in a position to share the actual findings of its investigations.

The probability of this type of resource being available from a benchmark partner is increasing as the number of organizations conducting formal benchmarking analyses continues to grow. Also, your chances of finding another organization that has already conducted some benchmarking analyses increase if you are benchmarking in topic areas that have attracted a considerable amount of attention from established benchmarkers (e.g., cycle time improvement and customer service-related subjects).

If a benchmark partner has conducted formal benchmarking investigations, it may be under some formal obligation to maintain the anonymity of its own benchmark partners. In that case, it may have to secure formal permission to discuss its findings with you, or it may direct you to the individuals with whom it has benchmarked. You may be asked to sign a nondisclosure agreement before the information can be made available to you and your organization.

Foreign Data Sources

One of the challenges of conducting best-practices benchmarking investigations is to expand the scope of your effort by including organizations outside the boundaries of your native country. Can an organization truly claim that it has found "world class" information if it has not expanded it's investigation to include any organization from around the world that may represent best practices? True, conducting best-practices investigations on a global scale can imply a tremendous amount of time and costs. However, available today are some excellent information sources that can add an international dimension to your search without your ever having to leave your own country. Experienced benchmarkers have had the advantage of building up their international resource directories over time. New benchmarkers, however, can learn from them by taking advantage of sources of international information that have proved useful and reliable.

■ *Banks.* Most major foreign banks have U.S. offices. Officers of these banks can provide useful information about organizations in their home lands, either directly or through their information libraries or databases, which are often accessible through their larger foreign branch locations. Before you approach such institutions, you should prepare a formal statement of your benchmarking intentions and perhaps even consider preparing a formal letter of introduction.

■ *Securities brokers.* Brokerage houses that employ specialists who focus on foreign companies are often willing to share information. In many cases these brokers maintain files that include extensive financial information on a select group of organizations. A good source for locating brokers and analysts is *Nelson's Directory of Investment Research*, W. R. Nelson Company, 1 Gateway Plaza, Port Chester, NY 10573.

■ *International Trade Commission (ITC).* The ITC maintains a database of foreign companies that U.S. companies are doing (or may want to do) business with. They also publish reports (often free) that cover a variety of subjects. Contact the ITC at 701 E Street NW, Washington, DC 20436.

■ *International Trade Administration (ITA).* The ITA, part of the U.S.

Commerce Department, is an excellent source of information about foreign markets. In particular, the ITA publishes *The Foreign Traders Index*, a database containing a wide range of information about foreign countries. Also, each of the ITA's country desk officers is an expert about a specific country, and can provide you with excellent leads. Request the *ITA Directory of Services and Employees* at the Department of Commerce, ITA, Washington, DC 20230.

■ *Consulates.* Many foreign consulates maintain extensive collections of information about companies in their native lands. They can also direct you to specific experts regarding the subject you are benchmarking. In some cases, it is advisable to approach a foreign consulate with a formal letter of introduction from either a senior staff member of your organization or from a foreign national or other individual who has an established relationship with the country in question.

U.S. consulates also provide useful assistance when you are trying to locate contacts or establish references in another country. The State Department publishes a "diplomatic list," which provides the names and addresses of U.S. embassy employees around the world. Contact the Superintendent of Documents, U.S. Government Printing Office, Washington, DC 20402. For international consulate information, request a copy of *UN Services and Embassies*, UN Public Inquiries Unit, Department of Public Information, United Nations, New York, NY 10013.

■ *Chambers of commerce.* Many foreign chambers of commerce publish directories that identify the location of U.S.-based branches of foreign companies.

■ *Library collections.* Many of the publications and directories you may be seeking are found only in libraries that specialize by country. The librarians can also provide you with good leads in tracking down information. Consult the White Pages in major city telephone books or ask for guidance from representatives from foreign consulates or large U.S.-based research libraries.

■ *Trade associations.* Trade associations may have data on foreign-based companies and may be able to identify foreign resources in their industries.

■ *The Office of Japan, Department of Commerce.* This office assists U.S. companies searching for information about Japan and Japanese companies. It has also provided benchmarkers with individuals in Japan to contact for benchmarking activities. Contact the Department of Commerce, International Trade Administration, Office of Japan, 14th Street and Constitution Avenue NW, Washington, DC 20230.

■ *On-line databases.* There are some excellent on-line databases that will provide you with sources of business-related information printed in foreign countries. An excellent English-language database covering Japanese business information is Japan Economic Newswire Plus. For information regarding organizations in Western Europe, try D&B International Market Identifiers. For information regarding these and other international database services, contact DIALOG, 3460 Hillview Avenue, Palo Alto, CA 94304.

Selecting Benchmark Partners—Take Advantage of the Opportunity

The benchmarking process presents an excellent opportunity to learn from best-practices companies. In most cases, those companies will cooperate with your benchmarking efforts, particularly if you approach them in an organized and professional manner. One of the deficiencies of many benchmarking efforts is a failure to take advantage of the opportunities that are presented by excellent companies. The fact is that even seasoned benchmarkers lose some momentum after a period of time and become lax in the process of investigating potential entries in the best-practices ranks.

Perhaps the most obvious indicator of a potential shortfall in your search for best-practices partners is the "brainstorm syndrome" described earlier. This is the process of a benchmarking team brainstorming best-practices companies, reducing the list of companies to a manageable number, and beginning the process of data collection. There is little or no effort to investigate other potential candidates for benchmarking, and no formal search is made of the traditional sources of information to validate and expand the choices the team has already proposed. Although the organizations identified may represent excellent practices, there is no attempt made to determine if these organizations truly represent *best* practices.

The brainstorm syndrome often tends to affect benchmarkers who have made rigorous attempts to identify best-practices companies. After some initial success, their next attempt may be more superficial and may not represent a thorough effort. These benchmarkers often incor-

Exhibit 5-4. The benchmarking process: Stage 3 diagnostics.

☐ You have allocated sufficient time on your benchmarking project calendar to allow you to investigate best-practices companies.

☐ You have secured the assistance of internal research services (e.g., libraries, technical centers) and/or you have secured the assistance of outside research services that can support your initial investigation process.

☐ You have identified specific information databases and other resources that have a direct bearing on your benchmarking investigation. These resources are known among your organization's benchmarking population.

☐ You have included information about resources available for investigating best-practices companies in your benchmarking training and communication activities.

☐ You have made an attempt to investigate nontraditional sources of best-practices companies; that is, you have made an attempt to expand your awareness of best practices by using resources that are new to you and your organization.

☐ You are not limiting your benchmarking attention to companies that fall into the "best-in-Cleveland" category, that is, those companies that are familiar, geographically convenient, or friendly to your organization.

rectly assume that they are not required to invest the same amount of effort in every benchmarking investigation. A sense of complacency may develop. This problem also affects individuals and teams that are using the process for the first time. Without any facilitation support or process discipline, these people are anxious to get started with the data-collection activities and they tend to hurry through this initial investigation stage. The results of this activity are often satisfying because the companies identified provide the teams with ideas that are new and different. Thus, the teams assume that they have done well because they have learned something new that can improve their own activities. But ask yourself, have these benchmarkers really optimized their opportunity to identify best practices? Will they ever return to the discipline of investigating best-practices companies if they have been rewarded by a much less rigorous process? Consider these questions as you review the Stage 3 diagnostics in Exhibit 5-4.

6

Stage 4: Collecting and Analyzing Benchmarking Information

Stage 4 of the benchmarking process involves the actual collection and analysis of benchmarking information (see Exhibit 6-1). It is assumed that you have already identified your benchmarking customers, their requirements, and the specific critical success factors (CSFs) that will constitute the core of your investigation; selected and trained the members of your benchmarking team; and identified an initial list of best-practices (or competitive) benchmark partners.

For many people who are new to benchmarking, the actual information-collection stage is the focus of their attention. In benchmarking seminars, participants are always anxious to get to this stage in the process—what they refer to as the "meat and potatoes" phase. This is understandable. The idea of interacting and visiting with other organizations is what attracts many organizations to the benchmarking process in the first place. Experienced benchmarkers, however, tell a different story. If the initial planning and preparation stages of the process have not been completed carefully, the process of collecting and analyzing benchmarking information can be unproductive or even counterproductive. In fact, when discussing benchmarking failures, experienced benchmarkers most often blame their difficulties on poor preparation during the planning stages and on being overanxious to begin the data-collection phase.

Exhibit 6-1. The benchmarking process: Stage 4.

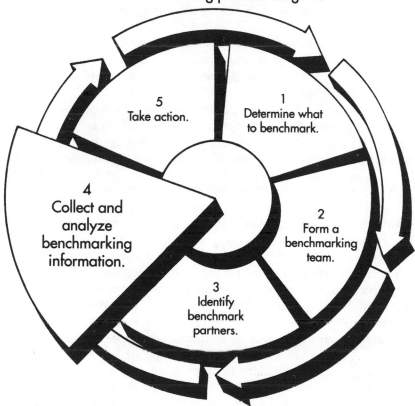

"Know Thyself"

One of the great philosophers posed the challenge to "know thyself." The process of understanding others begins with an understanding of the self. This philosophical theme serves the benchmarking process as well. One of the fundamental rules of benchmarking is to know your own processes, products, and services before you attempt to understand the processes, products, and services of another organization. Before you attempt to collect information about another organization, it is wise to collect and analyze information about your own internal operations. In many cases, this implies an internal benchmarking effort. In others, it may require only a simple measurement to document one's own activities.

Why is this so important? First, without a thorough investigation of your own internal products and processes, you may not realize the extent of your improvement opportunities. You may end up over- and underestimating your overall organizational position based on a limited awareness of the extent of your own internal activities. For example, without an accurate understanding of yourself, how can you calculate the potential gap that exists between your outcomes or activities and those of the best-practices organizations you have investigated? Second, without a thorough internal analysis, you may be bypassing some important internal benchmarking opportunities. You may never discover the possible sources of information and assistance available within your own organization. Third, when you begin investigating the activities of other organizations, they often ask you about your activities in the same area. If you are not prepared to respond with assurance regarding your own internal practices, you might give the impression that you are not fully prepared to investigate others, or you may appear to be collecting information out of sequence. The bottom line is you won't make a good impression.

Always ensure that your own organizational performance is well documented and understood before engaging in any external benchmarking activities. The desire to investigate and collect information about others often leads benchmarkers to delay their internal investigations or, in some cases, to skip the internal investigation altogether. Once this pattern is established, it can be difficult to regain the discipline needed to conduct a thorough internal appraisal. Other types of breakdowns in the benchmarking process are also prone to develop when an organization has not done a thorough job of self-analysis before benchmarking others.

In Chapter 2, it was noted that experienced benchmarking companies such as Alcoa, AT&T, and IBM treat the information-collection and analysis stages of their benchmarking models almost as a secondary factor. These companies are making a statement about the process of gathering benchmarking information. They are not trying to downplay the significance of information-collection practices; however, they are emphasizing the fact that collecting information is not difficult if the planning and preparation stages of the process are managed well and if the benchmarking participants are well schooled in the basic information-collection procedures and protocols.

The emphasis in this chapter is on effective information-collection and analysis practices. Experienced benchmarking companies use a limited number of information-gathering methods. Their experiences and recommendations regarding the use of these methods are reviewed, as well as the advantages and disadvantages of specific methods of information collection. Exhibit 6-2 presents a summary of the information-gathering methods discussed in this chapter.

Information Collection

Once you have determined the types of benchmarking information you need to collect and the information sources and organizations you will investigate, the next issue to consider is the data-collection methods you will use. The following methods of collecting benchmarking information are discussed in this chapter:

- Telephone interviews
- Personal meetings/site visits
- Surveys
- Publications/media
- Archival research

What factors determine the methods you use to gather benchmarking data? One key factor is driven by your customer requirements: the types of information needed, the proposed uses of the information, the level of detail required, and the quantity and quality requirements. Other factors involve levels of experience with certain information-gathering methods and personal or organizational preferences for using certain techniques. The following factors were cited most frequently by twenty-four experienced benchmarking companies:

- *Time constraints.* The amount of time available to collect information affects the number of sources that can be investigated and the methods used. For example, scheduling and conducting personal meetings is more time-consuming than interviewing over the telephone. Under strict time constraints, contact with employees of other organizations may have to be limited to telephone interviews.

Exhibit 6-2. Data-collection methods.

Method	Advantages	Disadvantages
Telephone interviews	• Easy to plan and conduct. • Enables contact with a large number of resources. • Can be conducted at almost any time. • Relatively inexpensive.	• "Cold calling" can be time-consuming. • Difficult to get return calls. • May be interruptions. • People are less likely to spend a lot of time on the telephone.
Personal meetings/site visits	• Establishes personal and professional relationship. • Provides more quality time. • Likely to produce a good deal of information.	• Expensive (travel costs). • Time-consuming. • There can be scheduling difficulties.
Surveys	• Ability to collect information from a large population. • Easy to construct. • Relatively inexpensive. • Easy transfer of information for analysis.	• Low return rate. • Impersonal. • No possibility to ask follow-up questions. • Questionable validity of some information. • Must be relatively brief. • Little possibility for detailed response.
Publications/ media	• Ease of collection/access. • Variety of resources. • Assistance available from data sources. • Inexpensive to collect. • Public access to information. • Large quantities of information produced for many types of industries.	• Overabundance of information in some industries. • Need to validate sources/statistics. • Many obscure references. • May be time-consuming. • Need to translate foreign material.
Archival	• Ease of collection (internal). • Inexpensive to collect.	• Missing data. • Poorly organized data. • May be time-consuming. • Often limited to internal analysis.

■ *Resource constraints*. The number and types of people and the amount of funding available to support the data-collection activities affect the methods used. For example, if there are no funds available for travel, the number of site visits may be severely restricted.

■ *Experience*. People tend to use data-collection methods that are familiar to them. For example, if members of a benchmarking team have extensive experience in telephone interviewing, that technique will most likely be their primary method of gathering information, as opposed to another method with which the group has little or no experience.

■ *Information-collection philosophy*. Based on information-collection experiences and the personal preferences of key internal benchmarking experts, most organizations develop an information-collection philosophy that is communicated in benchmarking orientation and process training sessions. This philosophy affects the methods used by benchmarking employees. For example, most experienced benchmarking companies (e.g., Xerox, AT&T, Du Pont, Caterpillar, IBM) express a strong preference for personal site visits with best-practices organizations. Their reasons, for the most part, have to do with the ability to ask detailed follow-up questions, the ability to pursue process questions in more detail, and the ability to develop closer personal relationships with employees from best-practices companies. Other companies, such as DEC, state a strong preference for telephone interviews or survey techniques, turning to site visits only as a last resort. That philosophy is based on DEC's successful experiences using those methods and a desire to maintain an economical approach to information collection.

Telephone Interviews

The telephone is the benchmarker's most valuable tool. In just a few minutes the caller can solicit answers to questions from a wide variety of sources. With some basic skill training, employees can become effective telephone interviewers and develop a high degree of efficiency in their information-collection activities.

There are several advantages to gathering information over the telephone. In general, telephone interviews are easy to plan and conduct. A basic outline and an ability to communicate are the primary requisites. Telephone interviews are also economical when a large number of contacts need to be made to collect information. Because of the different time zones, telephone interviewing extends a normal business day by three hours (within the continental United States). For example, benchmarkers on the East Coast can add three hours of telephone time to their schedules at the end of the normal workday in order to collect information from sources west of the eastern time zone. West Coast benchmarkers can get up early and begin the benchmarking day three hours before the normal workday begins. People in the central states really have it made; they can start early and end late. Although this sounds demanding, it does add some flexibility to the time available to collect information. International benchmarking creates additional opportunities to take advantage of time zone differences.

Telephones also provide flexibility regarding place. You can conduct a benchmarking interview from any telephone located anywhere—a hotel, a car, even an airplane (the most expensive benchmarking call I ever made). Another advantage is you don't have to be dressed in business attire to collect information over the telephone.

Difficulties in collecting information over the telephone often occur when the caller is insufficiently prepared. There are many horror stories regarding benchmarking "cold callers" who waste people's time talking in generalities, failing to adequately describe their mission and objectives, not properly identifying themselves, and intruding on people's schedules. It is also difficult to get people to return telephone calls, particularly if they have no advance warning of your purpose or you have left vague messages with their staff or on their answering machines. You are also more likely to be interrupted when speaking on the telephone; be prepared to be put on hold. Finally, people often limit the amount of time they will spend with you on the telephone at a single time. Generally, you would be doing well to get a good quality hour. You will probably have to call some of your sources several times to complete your information-collection activities, thus requiring you to play the usual game of "telephone tag" with your benchmark partners.

The following recommendations are made by those who are skilled and experienced using the telephone as a data-gathering tool:

■ *Prepare ahead of time.* Before you ever pick up a telephone, you should have a specific set of questions arranged in a logical sequence. You should also have some type of formal data-gathering outline that identifies the types of information to be recorded and provides space for recording the responses of each organization contacted (see Exhibit 6-3 for an example). If you have no experience collecting information in

Exhibit 6-3. Interview outline.

Name(s) of interviewer(s):	Lawrence Botticelli

Date: 6-30-92   Time: 1:15 pm

Organization: American Productivity Services, Inc.

Address: 10 Rogers Street

Cambridge, Mass.

Person contacted: Kim Bowers

Title: Manager, Executive Training

General topic: Management Training

Status of interview: Complete

1. ☐   Training costs
   - ☐ Number of trainers employed (salary + benefits)—internal
   - ☐ Overhead costs per class
   - ☐ Department travel expenses

   Notes:

2. ☐   Training budgets
   - ☐ Who develops budget?
   - ☐ What factors affect budget levels?
   - ☐ Percent of budget allocated to executive development
   - ☐ Projection of budget for next 3 years

   Notes:

this manner, take some time to practice speaking techniques, etiquette, and listening skills.

■ *Develop a list of preferred contacts.* Organize your resource list in order of preference and contact the organizations in that order. Make "call status" notations next to each resource you call (e.g., conducted interview, will return call, call back later).

■ *Coordinate your calling with other team members.* Ensure that only one team member is assigned to call each resource. Meet with team members to share information regarding your experiences to date. Check any internal benchmarking databases that list previous benchmarking contacts by organization and that provide summaries of previous benchmarking efforts that might be used as a reference. Make sure that you are aware of other individuals or teams from your organization that might be calling the same resources.

■ *Contact a specific individual.* By knowing the names and titles of knowledgeable sources, you avoid wasting time with someone who doesn't understand your need. When in doubt, ask for public relations or personnel (human resources). The public-relations department can generally put you in touch with the experts in the company as well as direct you to outside sources. Personnel usually has organizational charts handy and information regarding division or group locations.

■ *Explain who you are and why you are calling.* By doing so, you establish credibility and put the contact at ease. Prepare a written statement of your benchmarking activity, your own personal (or the team's) background, and a brief outline of the subjects you want to review. Send this information to your benchmark partner as part of your introduction—you can even fax this information while you speak on the telephone.

■ *Feed information.* Remember that you are calling people without warning. To help orient their thoughts and adjust their thinking toward your needs, share some of the information you have found out to date and tell them what you still need.

■ *Mention the source of your referral.* Referrals are door openers. Whenever you call someone based on a referral, make sure that the first thing you tell him or her is the name of the person who referred you. Be aware of previous benchmarking efforts that have involved the source's company, and refer by name to individuals who have cooperated with you or your organization in previous benchmarking situations.

■ *Exchange information.* Offer to exchange information or send a brief summary of the results. This is an especially effective technique when soliciting information from service professionals (e.g., marketing consultants, management consultants) who make their living dispensing advice. Many organizations will not give you information unless you can offer something in return.

■ *Give the other party a realistic estimate of the amount of time you require.* Never say that the interview will take a few minutes when an hour is more realistic. Acknowledge the time requirements and suggest multiple interviews as a way of coping with time constraints.

■ *Follow up.* Prepare a standard thank-you note to send to those individuals who have participated in your telephone interviews. A brief summary of project results or progress to date should also be included, if appropriate. Remember, you and your benchmarking team will probably be engaging in benchmarking projects in the future. As you begin to develop your benchmarking network, you should keep a file of contacts who have provided you with useful information. Following up with your benchmark partners is one way to begin to develop your own information network.

Personal Meetings/Site Visits

One of the most interesting and potentially rewarding experiences of benchmarking is the personal interview or site visit. In these situations, you arrange personal meetings with benchmarking resources and, if possible, arrange to conduct the meetings in their facilities. This type of data-collection method has several advantages. First, a personal meeting provides you with a better opportunity to gather more detailed information. In-person interviews almost always yield a higher quality of information than telephone interviews or surveys. Second, you may have the opportunity to observe the work process in action. Try to arrange a site tour with your benchmark partner and offer a reciprocal tour at your site. Third, personal meetings are more likely to result in the development of a long-term relationship with your benchmark partner than other forms of data gathering. There is really no substitute for a face-to-face meeting when establishing relationships with benchmark partners.

Other opportunities for face-to-face interactions occur at conferences, conventions, and trade shows. This type of meeting is useful when a benchmarking project is extended over a long period and there is no immediate need for information. Taking advantage of these opportunities may also save time and money with respect to the travel involved. Several experienced benchmarkers actually plan their benchmarking projects around the schedules of major conferences and conventions. They know that many of the best-practices contacts they wish to interview will be attending those meetings, and they target their personal interview times around the conference schedules.

Personal meetings and site visits do have two major drawbacks: They are time-consuming and, depending on the travel involved, expensive. One strategy to consider is to reserve personal meetings and site visits for those organizations that truly represent best practices or for direct competitors that have offered an invitation for a personal meeting. In other words, allocate your benchmarking resources wisely. Do not initiate a personal visit with every organization on your data-gathering list unless they are all highly select best-practices resources. For example, AT&T limits its site visits to the three or four organizations that present the best potential for collecting best-practices information. Du Pont uses the same strategy but encourages site visits to the top six or seven organizations. Xerox takes a more liberal position and encourages benchmarkers to visit as many organizations as is practical and necessary in order to collect the information needed to meet the customer's requirements.

There are some basic recommendations to consider when planning personal meetings or interviews:

■ *Confirm all appointments in writing.* This is a normal business courtesy and ensures that you have scheduled adequate time to conduct your interview. Follow up to confirm your appointment by telephone several days in advance of your meeting.

■ *Travel in pairs.* For very detailed or technical interviews that require extensive note taking, have another member of your benchmarking team accompany you. This allows for a constructive division of labor—one individual focusing on the interview and the other recording the information. The other person can also be useful as a source of validation regarding what was discussed. On site visits, you and your associate can split up and review more data or processes than one person could do alone.

Often the alternative to traveling in pairs is using a tape recorder.

This technique works well for some, but the process of listening to interview tapes and transcribing interview data can be frustrating and expensive for those who are not used to that particular technology. Also, most benchmarking companies discourage the use of tape recorders. They believe that tape recorders may intimidate benchmark partners or make them feel ill at ease.

■ *Use a structured outline.* As with telephone interviews, prepare your questions in advance. If possible, establish an interview matrix that lists the specific information you want to collect and provides space for entering the source of the information (see Exhibit 6-3). If appropriate, forward a copy of your questions or the data-collection form to the interviewee beforehand. This may save a lot of time for both of you.

■ *Arrange for a follow-up.* Even if you don't follow up in person or by telephone, it is recommended that you create an expectation that some level of follow-up may be required. This expectation facilitates any second-phase data gathering you may need to initiate.

■ *Send a thank you.* Acknowledge the meeting in writing or by telephone. Development of a personal benchmarking network is often affected by the level of professional courtesy and personal attention you show your benchmark partners.

Surveys

Surveys are often used as a means of collecting information from a large sample of individuals or organizations. They are most useful when collecting information that is easy for the respondent to provide and is not of a sensitive nature. The advantages of surveys are that they are relatively inexpensive to administer and summarize and they allow you to canvass a large audience in a short time. Many experienced benchmarking organizations use surveys as a method of narrowing their lists of potential benchmark partners. For example, if a specific set of CSFs has been identified and is capable of being measured by using a survey, the survey information can be examined to determine whether certain organizations stand out from the others on some characteristic. Those organizations can then be probed further, perhaps for more process information (i.e., how they were able to perform so well on the specific measures).

The disadvantages of surveys include their traditional low return rate and the fact that the information you can gather is limited. Surveys do not allow for follow-up questions or detailed process information. Also, constructing an effective survey requires a certain level of skill that is rare among people who have not been schooled in the practice of survey construction. In fact, there have been many reports of companies refusing to respond to surveys of any type due to a lack of survey quality.

There are some basic recommendations to consider when planning the use of surveys:

■ *Keep it short.* A rule of thumb is that people are willing to dedicate twenty to thirty minutes maximum to a survey they receive in the mail. If it takes longer than this to complete your survey, you can expect a reduced return rate.

■ *Call before you send.* If possible, call the individuals who will be receiving the survey. By requesting their cooperation and providing some basic information about your project, you significantly increase your return rate and might establish a rapport that could lead to further contact or site visits.

■ *Avoid lengthy response requirements.* Avoid questions that require the respondent to write lengthy responses. Limit the writing the respondent has to do to the minimum amount that still provides you with the information you need. Avoid open-ended questions.

■ *Provide a self-addressed, stamped return envelope.* This is a basic requirement.

■ *Identify yourself and how you can be reached.* Enclose a business card or telephone number where the respondents can reach you if they have any questions.

■ *Design your survey for easy data transfer.* Design your survey so that information can easily be transferred onto data summary sheets. For example, align the spaces used for recording responses in such a way that the response data are easy to read. Avoid crowding the document so that data are forced together. If possible, make use of some kind of data matrix that makes it easier for the respondents to record their information.

■ *Acknowledge receipt of the survey.* Send a response card back to the respondents (assuming that the survey is not anonymous) acknowledging your receipt of the survey and thanking them for their response.

Publications/Media

Choosing the publications you will review as part of your information search is sometimes difficult, given the number of resources that may be available. Most of the primary sources of information are readily identifiable and accessible: the well-known business, trade, and popular press sources that are commonly reviewed in your industry or functional specialty. The more difficult task is to consider those secondary sources that may be less known or harder to locate. Secondary sources are often recommended by others or mentioned as references by your primary sources. Given the amount of time it may take to locate secondary sources, you may have to limit your use of them. If your benchmarking team is familiar with any on-line databases for information in your subject area, a database search is often a good place to begin your review of publication and media resources.

Here are some basic recommendations for using publications and other media as a key information source:

■ *Avoid overlap.* Make sure that other members of your benchmarking team are not covering the same ground in the process of researching publications and media sources. Ensure that data-gathering assignments are clear before beginning the data search.

■ *Avoid rare documents.* Although some references seem attractive on paper, they may be difficult to locate, consuming a considerable amount of your research time to track down. Examples of rare documents include unpublished working papers, articles in defunct publications, esoteric academic works, foreign language resources, and transcripts of speeches delivered at meetings or conventions.

■ *Take advantage of staff support.* Use librarians, officials, managers, and other employees of publications and other media. Request their help in tracking down information and providing leads for locating information.

■ *Set up a document repository.* Develop a filing system for the printed materials you collect. Organize the files so that team members can easily access information collected by others. Attempt to integrate information that is collected with other information in your organization's files or library system. Consider developing an information index at the outset of your project.

■ *Develop a list of names of media resources.* Maintain this list of editors, publishers, librarians, and marketers for future use and possible follow-up regarding additional leads.

Archival Research

Archival research is typically used in the process of internal benchmarking. It consists of reviewing archival records in order to establish trends or examine the impact of changes in the business climate, the introduction of new technologies or products, and so on. Archival data are also useful to contrast information that has been collected from various organizational locations or divisions. In most cases, the information gathered through business archives is performance data, typically involving production, revenues, expenses, and critical incidents such as grievances, legal actions, and filings.

Here are some basic recommendations for using archival data as a resource:

■ *Combine archival data.* Combine these data with other information sources such as interviews. Archival data may be misleading if they are used without an understanding of the circumstances under which the information was collected. For example, a benchmarking team at IBM included extensive notes with a productivity trend analysis that covered a historical period dating back five years. A spike in the data indicated a severe increase in the number of problems uncovered with respect to a particular critical success factor. The attached notes indicated that those problems coincided with the first work-force reduction in the company's history.

■ *Set up an archive file.* Organize archival data for easy access and cross-referencing. Make sure that team members are familiar with the system used to organize information.

■ *Avoid overlap.* Make sure that members of your benchmarking team are not covering the same ground in the process of collecting archival information. Ensure that the data-gathering assignments are clear before beginning an archival data search.

Identify Your Information-Collection Strategy

Once your team has examined the potential methods of data collection, you need to allocate your benchmarking resources to optimize the results of your data-collection efforts. The objective of data collection is to produce the best information that will enable you to satisfy your customer requirements. These requirements often affect the types of information that need to be collected and thus the way in which it is collected. There are some basic considerations when identifying your information-collection strategy:

■ *Consider multiple methods of data collection.* The most effective information-collection strategy consists of a combination of personal and telephone interviews, site visits, the use of media resources, and an additional method such as surveys. The objectives of using multiple sources are to take advantage of the different kinds of information each resource provides and to develop a cross-referencing system. Most benchmarking efforts involve at least two methods of information collection. The exact methods used are affected by customer requirements, the scope of the project, the experience of the benchmarkers, and the information-collection philosophy of the organization.

■ *Conduct in-process reviews.* In the process of your data-collection efforts, take the time to consider the adequacy of the information sources that you have identified and make any changes to your strategy that might help improve your information-gathering results.

■ *Ensure that you have adequate resources to perform the task.* As a final consideration, make sure that your information-collection plan is not overly ambitious given your resource (time, people, and funding) limitations.

Benchmarking Protocol

When you are collecting information from a benchmark partner, there are some important issues to consider that might best be categorized as *protocol.* This term refers to professional etiquette or to some prescribed means of behavior. After having worked with dozens of benchmarking companies, I believe that some basic guidelines on professional benchmarking protocol are in order. Why? Primarily because so many benchmarking teams launch into the information-collection phase in a state of mild disorder. Although they may have a basic idea about their mission, customer requirements, and personal assignments, they are not quite ready to explain their objectives to others or to present themselves in a professional manner that will inspire the interest and confidence of prospective benchmark partners. This problem is becoming more widespread as the practice of benchmarking gains in popularity. Several large organizations—IBM, Xerox, Federal Express, and Motorola—that receive an incredible number of requests for information and benchmarking have begun to say no to benchmarking requests from companies that are not well prepared or have not given enough consideration to their time or information needs. A Xerox benchmarking specialist commented, "It's like they're doing us a favor by asking us to participate in their analysis!"

The following guidelines are based on the recommendations of companies that both benchmark and are asked to participate in the benchmarking projects of others. Consider adding a special section in your benchmarking curriculum regarding the issue of protocol. A few basic guidelines will serve your organization well as you begin to establish your own benchmarking network.

■ *Plan ahead; schedule realistically.* When you are benchmarking, you are asking others to cooperate with your information-gathering efforts. One of the more common problems in benchmarking project planning is inaccurate estimates of the time required to collect information from benchmark partners. Many organizations assume that collecting information from others is similar to collecting information internally. This is a bad assumption. A basic rule is to estimate the amount of time you think is reasonable with respect to your information-collection activities, then double it. Although this estimate may seem unreasonable, it will probably be fairly accurate. Remember that you are going to have to conform to the schedules of a number of other organizations. Your benchmarking priorities are not their priorities. They may take longer than expected to collect the information you request. Information validation and callbacks to fill in the holes may cause delays you had not anticipated. After you have completed several cycles of benchmarking, you will be able to gauge your time requirements more accurately. As you begin the process, however, be careful when scheduling your project; your traditional assumptions of time requirements don't apply.

■ *Prepare a briefing package.* Before you contact benchmark partners (both internal and external), prepare a benchmarking project briefing package for your benchmark partners. It will help them understand your information needs and, in turn, help them do a better job of preparing for your information-collection activities. A practical briefing package includes the following:

—A statement of purpose outlining your information needs and the reasons for initiating the contact.

—A personal introduction explaining your role in the benchmarking process.

—A general description of the benchmarking project, including anticipated results, expected project times, and resource requirements.

—A list of other benchmark partners that have agreed to participate in your investigation.

—A specific description of your exact information needs from the organization you are contacting.

—A benchmarking subject outline of the information you require from the partner. This might be a list of critical success factors in the order they will be addressed in the interview.

—An indication of the specific type of follow-up they should expect from you or that you expect of them.

—Any statements pertinent to the issue of confidentiality, anonymity, or legal assurances regarding your joint participation in the process.

—Telephone and fax numbers where they can contact you or your team members.

Realistically, your briefing package should be about two pages long plus whatever information outlines you need to attach.

■ *Ease your way in.* Bold and aggressive strategies for making initial contact with potential benchmark partners tend to irritate rather than motivate. Many benchmarking requests sound like demands or are treated as entitlements. Remember, you are asking people—in many cases strangers—to go to some length to participate in your investigation. Your approach should be respectful of their interests and their calendar.

One approach that works well is to make the initial contact with prospective partners over the telephone. Briefly introduce yourself and describe the nature of your project and what information you need. All you are attempting to do at this point is to solicit interest in your investigation. If a potential partner shows interest, suggest that you fax a copy of your benchmarking briefing package. Faxing the package immediately capitalizes on the prospect's initial interest in the project. Any time lag of a week or two decreases the potential partner's enthusiasm. After you fax the package, follow up with a phone call in order to clarify the information and to give the prospective partner an opportunity to ask questions. The briefing package also enables the prospective partner to estimate how long it will take to assemble the information. As aggressive as this may sound, it is mellow compared to some of the pressure tactics that have been reported by people contacted for benchmarking purposes.

■ *Use a top-down contact strategy.* Use a top-down approach to initiate contact with your benchmark partners. Contact functional managers at a fairly high organizational level and work your way down the functional hierarchy to the individuals you need to contact. There are several advantages to this approach. First, there is an element of professional courtesy that is evident by working your way through the formal channels of the organization. If you are benchmarking information that might be considered sensitive, this is very important. Second, a more senior person might be able to refer you to multiple sources of information in the organization and introduce you to employees you may not have thought to contact on your own. Third, working your way down through the organizational hierarchy often provides you with referrals from senior-level managers. These referrals will generally elicit a greater level of interest from employees who report through those senior-level managers. Finally, remember that you are always looking for opportunities to establish long-term partnerships with functional experts in best-practices companies. Establishing contact at the higher levels of those organizations may be instrumental in building a foundation for constructive long-term relationships.

■ *Stick to your outline.* When you interview or survey your benchmark partners, stick to the agreed-upon outline you provided them as part of your initial inquiry. Do not attempt to introduce new topics in the middle of an interview or ask for new information when you arrive at a site. Many organizations are reluctant to respond to questions that deviate from the agreed-upon outline. One benchmarking specialist at Xerox and another at DEC are so tired of being badgered for additional information that they refuse to have dinner with benchmarkers who continually probe for information.

■ *Limit the size of your site visit team.* Keep the size of your site visit team to one or two people. A large group is not necessary for an effective site visit. When you schedule more than two people for a site visit, you usually force your partner to locate the meeting in a conference room or similar facility—not an optimal setting for a site interview. It is best to conduct your interview as close to the actual work setting as possible (consider the possibilities for additional contacts).

Information Organization

At this point in the benchmarking process you assemble your raw data and organize the information in a way that enhances its utility and meaning. What may seem like a huge collection of facts can become a revelation about a significant business event, a trend in business practices or products, or a profile of business results. Data organization and analysis are not difficult if you design your data-collection and organization strategy *before* you begin your information-collection activities. The following recommendations can help you plan your data-collection and analysis activities.

Start With an Outline

Organize your data collection around a topic outline that lists the specific subjects of your benchmarking activities. In Chapter 3, the level of specificity of information was discussed. Level-one information is very broad—for example, the name of an organization or function to be benchmarked. Level two is more specific and defines aggregate data categories or broad areas of focus—budgets, numbers of employees, number of items in a catalog, and so on. Level three is very specific and focuses on measures that might be available only from the actual data source—actual costs (as a percentage of revenue), process issues, specific growth plans, and the like. The data-collection outline should use these information levels as a guideline. For example, let's examine Exhibit 6-3. The level-one measure is management training, listed next to the words "General Topic." The level-two measures include information such as "training costs," which is followed by a detailed listing of specific costs to be measured—number of trainers (salary, benefits cost), overhead costs per class, and travel budgets. These are the level-three measures.

Note that the interview outline also includes an introductory section that provides space for the interviewer to record the source of the interview information and the status of the interview. This is a useful record of interviews conducted by the benchmarking team, and such information can easily be transferred to a computerized summary system to record basic information about completed interviews or interviews in progress.

These outlines have several distinct uses. First, they help the benchmarking team develop a meaningful and organized set of questions regarding the critical success factors that have been identified. As information is collected, the outline can be used as a guide to record information in an organized manner. Also, as the members of a benchmarking team attempt to summarize the information from their respective interviews, an outline enables large quantities of information to be sorted and recorded with a high degree of efficiency and accuracy. Second, the outline serves as a preview of the subjects you want to benchmark with your prospective partners. This type of outline, included in a basic briefing package, provides a realistic overview of the subject to be investigated. If the outline is specific, the benchmark partner may have enough information to begin the process of collecting information and preparing responses to your questions.

Use an Information Matrix

An information matrix is simply a tool that identifies the information you are collecting (identified from your outline) and the reported facts as gathered from the organizations or individuals you are benchmarking. These types of matrixes can be used during the actual process of collecting information along with an interview outline.

Information matrixes help you organize your data-collection and reporting efforts and provide your benchmarking team with a consistent method of data collection and organization. Also, matrixes simplify the process of consolidating information from multiple sources over time.

Exhibit 6-4 is an example of a typical information matrix. This particular matrix records information collected from six organizations on the subject of factors affecting sales rep productivity. The rows of the matrix list the six organizations that participated in the benchmarking investigation, beginning with information from the company conducting the benchmarking investigation ("Benchmarking Organization"). The remainder of the companies are recorded as letters B through F.

Exhibit 6-4. Benchmarking information matrix.

Factors Affecting Sales Rep Productivity

	Estimated Direct Sales Cost*	Average Accounts per Salesperson	Commission/ Bonus as a % of Total Pay	Sales Support Personnel per Rep	Sales Reps per Manager
Benchmarking organization	6.1%	60	10%	1:1	6:1
B	6.1%	70–80	10%	1.5:1	5:1
C	7.0%	70	10%	1.2:1	6:1
D	5.0%	50	30%	1.5:1	5:1
E	4.6%	25–30	0%	1.8:1	8:1
F	7.2%	40–60	0%	.8:1	4:1

*As percent of revenues.

This is an example of what is called a blind study, in which the organizations participating in the investigation are not identified.

The five columns of the matrix record information about the five specific topics measured. Note the utility of the matrix. A simple review of the information in the columns allows the benchmarker to identify trends or numbers that indicate potential for further investigation. Also, as the members of the benchmarking team record their responses on these types of matrixes, the information can easily be summarized and tabulated in the form of summary matrixes.

Analyze in Phases

One of the realities of organizing benchmarking information is that you may have to consider or interpret the information you collect in phases. For example, suppose you have identified six organizations that represent best practices in your particular area of interest—for instance, scrap rate reduction. During phase one, you and your team conduct interviews with each of these organizations over the telephone and enter some of that information on a basic information matrix (see Exhibit 6-5). When you review this matrix, it is apparent that two of the six benchmark partners (B and E) have significantly lower scrap rates than the others in the best-practices category. You then decide to pursue process questions (i.e., how they do it) with those two organizations that appear to have an advantage over the others included in the investigation— phase two.

Phase two includes more thorough interviews with those two benchmark partners, perhaps even site visits. Therefore, a preliminary analysis of some of the information provided by best-practices organizations has led to more data collection. Such a basic review of preliminary information matrixes may highlight organizations that should receive preferential consideration as your benchmarking team investigates the specific processes of excellent companies.

Summarize Your Data

Once you and your benchmarking team have completed your data-collection assignments, the next task is to summarize the information collected. The most straightforward way to accomplish this task is to develop another set of information matrixes that summarize the information. In most cases, these matrixes are simply extended versions of

Exhibit 6-5. Phase one benchmarking matrix.

	Scrap Rate (%)	Correct Shipments (%)	On-Time Delivery (%)
Your organization	5.0	93	90
A	7.3	97	88
B	**1.2**	96	97
C	3.9	91	95
D	4.4	98	93⁻
E	**1.1**	94	97
F	6.1	93	98

those used by individual members of the benchmarking team. In other cases, such as when each member of the team was responsible for a unique data set, the summary report is simply the assembled matrices of the team members.

In addition to the summary sheets, you may want to include narratives. These narratives provide additional detail about the process of data collection, the sources that were used, problems encountered in the data-collection process, and other information that supplements the matrices. If you are going to include narratives in your data summary and analysis, make sure that you provide your team with a standard format and examples of how the narratives should be structured—their length, level of detail, and so on.

Information Analysis

After your information has been collected and summarized, you are ready for the next step in the benchmarking process—data analysis. Consider the following recommendations as you begin the process of determining the meaning of the information you have collected.

Check for Misinformation

Misinformation is information that is incorrect due to such factors as misinterpretation, improper recording or transcription, purposeful misrepresentation of data (from the source), and errors (from the source). Misinformation may be difficult to identify by simply reviewing the data summaries—subtle differences in facts may be hard to spot. There are, however, clues that can indicate misinformation in your data. One indicator is information that deviates significantly from what was expected or from other data that should be comparable. For example, one matrix of hourly wage rates demonstrated a discrepancy of almost 30 percent for one organization. The discrepancy was explained when it was learned (via a follow-up call) that benefits costs were included in the particular wage statistic. Another indicator of possible misinformation is conflicting data from multiple sources—for example, information collected on the same subject by different members of the team or by different means (e.g., interviews, published reports). This is a more common indicator of misinformation. Of course, some allowance must be made for minor differences in data collected from different sources. However, major discrepancies (based on your own definition of major) should be investigated.

If there is any indication of misinformation in your data, consider taking the following actions. First, recheck your sources for accuracy and make any necessary corrections. Second, if your sources continue to provide conflicting information, you can attempt to reconcile the differences by informing your sources of the conflict and asking for their help to resolve the issue. You can also identify alternative sources that may be more accurate (in some cases, this may mean using a more rigorous means of data collection, such as interviews with the sources). Third, if rechecking the data is not worth the time or effort required, simply eliminate the data from the database.

One major caution: If you discover that misinformation is a common factor in your database, you may have to reexamine your data-collection strategy and consider alternative strategies or methods.

Identify Patterns

This is one of the most basic forms of analysis you will conduct. General patterns or trends are often noticeable as you examine your data matrices. For example, trends in sales data reported by year for a set of competitors are often noticeable when the data are arranged in a matrix. Cost and revenue data are generally analyzed immediately for patterns or trends.

Identify Omissions or Displacement

What is *not* present after you have completed your analysis can often be as significant as what *is* present. Problems in this area usually consist of two major types. The first is one of omission—missing data that should be available. Although some data are difficult to collect and interpret, other pieces of information should be available—for example, information on employee demographics, such as education level or geographical location. Omission of these kinds of data is worth exploring. The second type of problem is called displacement and often involves significant changes in data trends without explanation. For example, an organization may provide information that represents a radical departure from its normal or expected routine (e.g., pricing practices, warranty provisions). This information may even be cross-checked and found to be accurate. The lack of an explanation (or narrative) for this type of puzzling data is considered a displacement. If you discover such displacements in your data, consider cross-checking your sources for accuracy or providing a narrative explanation to accompany the data.

Check Out-of-Place Information

Some information that you discover about other organizations just won't seem to "fit" with respect to other information you have collected—or it may noticeably deviate from the information you thought you would find. For example, one organization that was benchmarking the subject of management training asked some specific questions about how many hours a year were allocated to formal management training. Eight of the best-practices organizations surveyed averaged thirty-eight hours per year, with a range from twenty-four to sixty hours. However, the ninth organization surveyed reported its average to be 120 hours. This response seemed out of place—twice the number of hours spent by the company reporting the second-highest total.

When faced with such an out-of-place response, you have three choices: (1) Accept the information literally as reported; (2) reject the information as being unrealistic or untrue; or (3) follow up with the organization reporting the out-of-place information so you can validate the information in question. Obviously, choice number three is recommended.

In many cases, the out-of-place information is caused by a misunderstanding on the part of the benchmark partner; that is, it hasn't understood the question. Once the misunderstanding is cleared up, the partner is often able to respond more realistically and in a manner more in line with reasonable expectations. In the example of the ninth organization cited earlier, the 120 hours allocated to formal management training was not accurate; included was information that should not have been entered into the calculation (off-site business meetings were counted as training hours). However, where the information in question turns out to have been reported correctly, you have the opportunity of investigating the information more carefully.

Occasionally, checking this type of information may bring to light a discrepancy of opinion or fact for the benchmark partner. That is, when attempting to validate the benchmarking information, there may be some level of disagreement within the partner's organization regarding the "correct response." In these situations, let the benchmark partner determine the correct response and report it back to you, explaining the nature of the discrepancy if appropriate. You can often assist in this process by ensuring that your questions are well-understood by your benchmark partner.

In summary, the best course of action to take when you discover out-of-place information is to investigate further with your benchmark partner. Simply accepting the information as valid or rejecting it as unrealistic are not recommended courses of action.

Draw Conclusions

The ultimate goal of benchmarking analysis is to better understand relevant activities of other organizations and use that information to improve your own organizational performance. In most benchmarking analyses, you review information that was gathered from a number of organizations. One of the most difficult challenges is to make logical comparisons and draw reasonable conclusions from information that, in some cases, may seem contradictory or confusing. At the very least, some of the information you collect from your benchmark partners will force you to challenge your assumptions or question the practices of your partners. For example, if you are trying to determine what certain competitors or best-practices companies do under certain circumstances, your goal is to understand how those organizations think and how they manage their business (in a strategic planning sense). The decisions and business practices of your benchmark partners are based on their history and experience, their assumptions, their corporate culture, and how they perceive their competitive environment. To you, their perceptions may not be realistic or reasonable, but that is not important in a benchmarking analysis. The issue is what the other organization perceives and does. Your challenge is to interpret those activities in relation to your own history, experience, assumptions, and the like. Too often, benchmarkers impose their own normative judgments on the decisions and actions of others. Be careful of this tendency. Benchmarking is not an ideal forum for expressing personal opinion or for critiquing the actions of others. It is suited for investigating the products and processes of others and learning from that exposure to new ideas.

The data-evaluation process involves collecting the facts and eliminating unreliable, inaccurate, false, and irrelevant data. You organize and assemble the useful data and look for patterns that reveal trends and business developments. Then you draw inferences about the actions, strategies, plans, and results of other organizations. Finally, you are ready to draw conclusions based on the information you have collected.

The levels of analysis and types of conclusions that organizations make as a result of their benchmarking activities generally fall into several categories:

■ *Documenting your own internal processes.* One of the most useful by-products of the benchmarking process is the intense internal analysis that precedes the external benchmarking effort. For many organizations, this may present a unique opportunity to step back from their day-to-day operations and focus significant attention to the intricacies of their own processes. For example, when some benchmarking organizations use process mapping, they are able to trace the specific steps in processes that have never been formally documented. Others are able to reengineer some of their core business processes. And for a few, benchmarking presents a method of bringing internal experts together in a cooperative effort that may be unique to their organizational culture.

Internal process analysis helps you develop your internal benchmarking contacts and form internal networks. At the very least, it allows you to identify other employees or teams that could benefit from your benchmarking efforts, spreading the benefit and compounding the advantages that the overall organization receives from your efforts. The best case is that you not only identify others who could benefit from your efforts but find willing internal partners who want to actively participate in your benchmarking activities.

■ *Knowing your strengths and weaknesses.* A fundamental outcome of most benchmarking investigations is an understanding of your strengths and weaknesses. This information often comes from those who know your operation—your employees, customers, suppliers, competitors, and competitors' customers. Other perspectives about your organization may be provided by your benchmark partners. Even though you are investigating the best practices of others, you will receive a fair amount of feedback about your own organization as you collect information. Such feedback can be revealing, frightening, or satisfying, but this type of information exchange requires an open mind and a willingness to accept the opinions of others. In many cases, this information is some of the most meaningful and energizing to the benchmarking organization.

■ *Determining the performance gap.* One of the more traditional objectives of a benchmarking investigation involves a comparison between your organization's products, services, work processes, or results and those of your competitors or excellent or best-practices organizations. The objective of this analysis is to identify any type of performance gap that exists. For the most part, attention is focused on negative gaps—that is, when your performance, products, or services are operating at a level below that of the organizations you have benchmarked. Of course, there may be situations or areas of activity in which your organization has an advantage or is clearly superior (producing a positive gap). However, these situations do not tend to interest benchmarkers.

Consider the graph in Exhibit 6-6. This example shows the trends in research and development (R&D) spending (reported as a percentage of sales) for four organizations: the organization conducting the benchmarking activity, two competitors, and one company identified as a world-class organization. This type of graph can often be constructed by transferring data directly from the data summary sheets that were used in the data-collection process. What does this information tell you? First, there is definitely a gap in the level of R&D spending among the various organizations, with the world-class organization leading both of the competitors, and all three other organizations outspending the benchmarking company. Second, note that there is a definite trend toward a gradual increase in R&D spending as a percentage of sales. This graph also shows the average gap between the benchmarking company and its benchmark partners over the five-year period from 1985 through 1989. The 1.1 percent competitors' average was calculated by averaging the annual differences between the benchmarking company and the two competitors over the five-year measurement period. Likewise, the 2.9 percent world-class average is the average difference in R&D spending between the benchmarking company and the world-class organization over the same five-year period.

However, before concluding that the R&D spending gap depicted in Exhibit 6-6 indicates a negative result (again, the tendency to attach a normative interpretation to benchmark data), one should consider the following qualitative factors:

- The amount of yield from R&D spending. How efficient are the R&D processes in these organizations? How effective are these R&D dollars?
- The relative size of the organizations, the extent of their product lines, their other sources of revenue (e.g., a parent company), and so on. Are there factors that make comparisons of these numbers like comparing apples and oranges?
- How does this statistic correlate with other bottom-line measures,

Exhibit 6-6. The performance gap.

Issue: R&D spending as a percentage of sales, 1985–1989

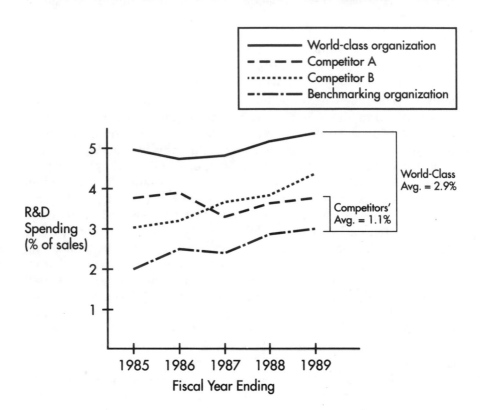

such as market share, profitability, and growth? The relationship may be weak, or there may even be a negative correlation.

The message here is simple: Before attempting to draw conclusions from the results of benchmarking data, consider the various factors that might affect the interpretation of those numbers. (See Exhibit 6-7 for a summary of the information-collection and analysis recommendations and Exhibit 6-8 for the Stage 4 diagnostics.)

Exhibit 6-7. Information collection and analysis.

Process Recommendations	Analysis Outcomes
▪ Use a data-collection outline.	▪ Satisfy customer requirements.
▪ Use information matrices.	▪ Define your competitive advantage.
▪ Develop a data-collection calendar.	▪ Identify the business context.
▪ Summarize data (matrixes).	▪ Know your organization's strengths and weaknesses.
▪ Check for misinformation.	▪ Determine your competitors' strengths and weaknesses.
▪ Identify data patterns.	▪ Determine the performance gap.
▪ Identify omissions/ displacement.	
▪ Check for anomalies.	
▪ Exercise care when interpreting numerical or statistical data.	

Exhibit 6-8. The benchmarking process: Stage 4 diagnostics.

☐ Information-collection methodologies have been identified with respect to time and resource constraints as well as benchmarking team experience and preferences.

☐ Information-gathering protocol has been developed and reviewed with team members.

☐ Structured interview outlines are prepared prior to any benchmarking activity.

☐ Your internal research/library staff (or an equivalent staff at a major library) has been informed of your benchmarking information needs and has been briefed on the benchmarking process.

☐ Your information-collection strategy emphasizes multiple methods of information collection (e.g., telephone interviews, site visits, surveys).

☐ Your organization (or benchmarking team) has secured sufficient resources to enable you to conduct a thorough and meaningful benchmarking investigation.

☐ You have collected internal benchmarking information before beginning the process of benchmarking on the outside.

☐ Your team has prepared a briefing package for use with prospective benchmark partners.

☐ Your team is well acquainted with the construction and use of information matrices.

☐ Your team has attempted to evaluate benchmarking information in phases.

☐ You have checked your benchmarking information for patterns, misinformation, omissions, and so on.

☐ Your team acts with caution when interpreting benchmarking information that is in the form of numbers, averages, and so on.

7

Stage 5: Taking Action

The primary objective of benchmarking is to take action (see Exhibit 7-1). Although benchmarking is a process of investigation, the motivation for initiating an investigation in the first place is to stimulate and support change. Interestingly, when discussing this part of the benchmarking process with those organizations that have a tremendous amount of experience with the process, the organizations all agree that this particular stage is the least complicated and the most straightforward. Their reasons go back to Stage 1 of the benchmarking process. That is, the process of benchmarking is driven by a desire to take action, a rigorous set of customer requirements, and an identification of specific critical success factors that serve as the focus of the investigation. The benchmarkers at DEC probably said it best when they stated that they encourage a benchmarking investigation only *after* the decision has been made to take action. DEC is not about to get into the business of generating benchmarking reports that get forwarded to an in-basket somewhere. DEC advocates an action-oriented process that leads to change. Many other benchmarking organizations agree with DEC's position, so for many of the best-practices benchmarking companies, the final stage of the process is almost a preordained event. As the benchmarker at DEC noted, "It just becomes a question of developing an implementation plan."

There are several basic kinds of activities that can take place at the action stage of the benchmarking process (Exhibit 7-2). These activities are reviewed in this chapter. A key point to remember is that there should be few surprises as you reach the end of the benchmarking process. If you have followed the process closely with a fair amount of

Exhibit 7-1. The benchmarking process: Stage 5.

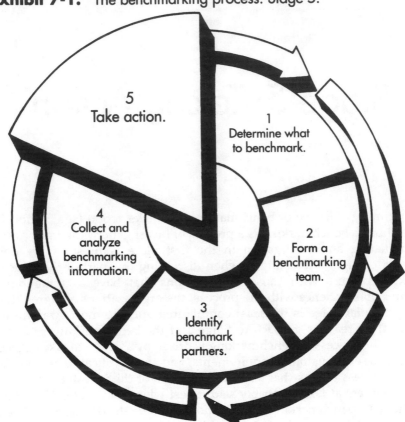

discipline, you should be comfortable with your progress and your results as you complete the benchmarking cycle. The following actions that typify Stage 5 of the benchmarking process are not presented in any particular order. For many organizations, there is an attempt to take action on all of the items reviewed here. Other organizations may attempt to accomplish only one or two. But remember, as long as the benchmarkers are satisfying their basic customer requirements and producing useful information, the process can be considered a success.

Exhibit 7-2. Action plan.

- Produce a benchmarking report/summary.
- Present findings to benchmarking customers.
- Communicate findings.
    - —Internal—other functional groups
    - —Benchmark partners
- Look for opportunities.
    - —Product/process improvement
    - —Learning—bring new ideas and concepts into your organization
    - —Forming functional networks
- Encourage recycling efforts.
    - —Modify/improve your use of the process.
    - —Introduce new/related subjects for benchmarking.

Producing a Benchmarking Report

Producing benchmarking reports is a typical activity when the customer of the benchmarking information is a commissioning manager. From the outset, these types of benchmarking teams have as an objective the production and delivery of a project report. In some cases, this is a one-time activity similar to a task force or task team assignment. In other situations, the benchmarking team prepares a report in order to fulfill an obligation to the various benchmark partners who agreed to participate in the investigation partly because they expected to receive a summary of the findings at the end of the project cycle.

After the basic analysis has been completed, the final major task of the benchmarking team is to generate a report. This report is intended to serve the following purposes:

- As a report to be delivered to the benchmarking customers
- As a summary of the data that were collected and analyzed
- As a record of the organizations benchmarked and key project contacts
- As a communications product for other internal employees and functions

- As the foundation for communications to external parties
- As a record for the organization's benchmarking database and files

Report Contents

The following is a comprehensive table of contents for a benchmarking report. This level of reporting may not be required if the benchmarking analysis is a part of an ongoing data-collection effort. In that case, a condensed version of the report might be called for.

- *Statement of need/purpose.* This is a statement of the motivation for conducting the benchmarking analysis. For example, the organization is considering expanding into new markets or investing in new technologies. This section should present any data or incidents that have been instrumental in stimulating the benchmarking effort. A historical perspective on an issue is often useful as part of the introduction, and the report should include dates to identify the time frame.

- *Project customers.* Identify the project customers by job title; name is optional. Identify any information partners that may be cooperating in joint analyses. If a team has proactively sought out customers (e.g., secondary customers) for its benchmarking work, the process for identifying and contacting these potential customers should be recorded.

- *Customer requirements.* List the customer information requirements, including project scope, benchmarking subjects identified, requirements for information quantity and quality, delivery dates, and format requirements.

- *Project team.* Identify project team members by name, organization, job title, and work address. As an option, explain the selection process for team members. Identify significant project support personnel.

- *Team process.* Describe the process of team orientation and training. Describe the amount of time each member dedicated to the task. Identify specific roles and responsibilities taken on by team members. Identify key decisions made by the team regarding the team process (e.g., use of interviewing teams, processes for data review and process correction).

- *Project calendar.* Display the project calendar, noting key dates for key meetings, reporting activities, report completion, and other events worth noting.

■ *Subjects benchmarked.* Present a data outline that lists general categories of information and specific measures used to gather information.

■ *Information sources.* List information sources by type. Identify specific references for printed material. List names of individuals contacted, organizations, and job titles. Consider constructing an information sources index that summarizes the resource information.

■ *Methodology.* Describe the methods used for collecting data—interviews, surveys, printed materials search, and so on. Include copies of surveys or questionnaires as an appendix to the report. Include copies of the project calendar, if appropriate.

■ *Results/summary.* Include a data summary in the form of narratives, summary matrices, or both. Include a description of the summary matrices design. Organize the narrative according to the data outline that was used to gather the information. Include any large volumes of raw data as appendices to the report.

■ *Narrative.* Provide any additional narrative that may be required to describe miscellaneous topics regarding the benchmarking investigation, such as additional data gathered in the process, difficulties encountered, or outstanding events that might be of interest to readers of the report.

■ *Analysis.* Present charts and narrative that describe the analysis of the data. Include any graphs or charts that help illustrate the results. Avoid technical details regarding quantitative analysis, or include this type of information as an appendix.

■ *Results.* Present the results in summary fashion and provide an accompanying narrative if required. Refer to the original customer requirements when presenting the results summary. Keep the results section factual. Consider the use of an executive summary or results summary that captures the key results on a few pages.

■ *Next steps.* Provide any information regarding the next steps of the benchmarking process. For example, note any follow-up data collection that is planned and provide a calendar of expected activities and completion dates. Discuss any implications for further benchmarking analysis that were identified during the course of the project.

In general, benchmarking reports of this scope are becoming rare because many benchmarking teams are action-oriented and would rather not invest inordinate amounts of time producing extensive reports. These types of detailed reports are typical of task force and task team benchmarking activities where the project sponsor expects a detailed report of the entire process.

Presenting Findings to Benchmarking Customers

In some situations, the benchmarking team is required (or requested) to deliver a presentation to its customers. These customers may include groups of managers, other teams within the organization, or a single commissioning manager. Such a presentation is an oral version of the benchmarking report; in many cases, both a verbal and a written report are required. These presentations also provide the customers with an opportunity to ask questions. The benchmarking team members may elect a spokesperson or a small group of spokespersons in order to keep the presentation manageable. These verbal benchmarking reports may vary in length from an hour (executive briefing) to a full day (including discussion).

Benchmarking reports and presentations offer an opportunity to expand the audience for the benchmarking findings and stimulate action to initiate change. In some organizations, these presentations are also used as opportunities to acknowledge or reward the efforts of the benchmarking team members.

The benchmarking team may also communicate its findings to other members of the organization, either directly through written memos to select groups of employees or indirectly by means of other communications vehicles, such as newsletters or on-line systems created especially for that purpose. Xerox, in conjunction with its quality activities, sponsors events such as Teamwork Days, which are massive regional fairs that give teams the opportunity to share their work as problem solvers and benchmarkers with other employees, customers, and suppliers. The value of any benchmarking activity can be increased by sharing the results of the benchmarking effort with others who can benefit from the findings and recommendations. Most organizations that have established a stable benchmarking process record benchmarking summaries onto an on-line system that can be accessed by any employee. New teams are encouraged to check the system for benchmarking results that may affect their projects and to look for leads and benchmarking contacts as they prepare to launch their team activities.

Identifying Possible Product and Process Improvements

One of the key activities of a benchmarking team is to find opportunities for product and process improvement. During the course of benchmarking projects, teams will be exposed to all kinds of new ideas, and the temptation to take immediate action based on early findings is strong. By the time a benchmarking team reaches Stage 5, the challenge is to sort through a variety of improvement possibilities and decide which ideas, concepts, and suggestions make the most sense to incorporate into the business environment.

Benchmarking teams have to decide what action they will take as a result of their benchmarking activity. Often, they close the loop and go back to their original customer requirements and reassess any implementation and improvement plans based on the following factors:

■ *Customer requirements revisited.* Have the customer requirements remained stable, or has a new set of requirements been added to the original plan?

■ *Funding.* What level of financial (or human resources) support is available to support the team's recommendations?

■ *Time.* How much time does the team have available to incorporate change into the environment? What pressures is the organization putting on the team in terms of other work priorities, new assignments, or other benchmarking initiatives?

■ *Interest/energy level.* Has the team sustained its energy level during the process cycle? Are team members capable of carrying out the total assignment, or are they burned out after the investigation phase?

■ *Original product/process improvement assumptions.* Has anything changed in the organizational environment since the team started the benchmarking activity? Has the original need decreased or increased dramatically? Have any of the primary customers for the benchmarking information changed? Has the organization been faced with another challenge or opportunity that places the team's efforts on the back burner?

Based on these factors, the team either continues with its original project plan or adjusts it accordingly. Teams always feel the pressure of time; they are always trying to move the process along as quickly as possible, sometimes to the detriment of the process itself. Team members know that things change so rapidly in the business environment that every month they spend on a project is another month that could alter their ability to apply the benchmarking information to the work situation.

Improvement Outcomes

The majority of product and process improvements made by benchmarking teams generally involve one or more of the following improvement outcomes:

■ *Product/process improvements*. At this stage, benchmarkers use the benchmarking information to alter their actual products or processes. These alterations may be subtle or dramatic. Teams must also face reality regarding the amount of time and resources it will take to implement the changes.

For some benchmarkers, the process of incorporating change is dramatic and rapid. Once the decision is made and the resources are in place, the changes take place almost immediately. This type of improvement was demonstrated by a team that had investigated the process of coating special lenses. It turned out that their inefficiencies (and, therefore, their opportunities) were greatly affected by the dated technology they were using. The process improvement that was identified involved purchasing a new piece of equipment—which had just been approved in the budget plan. This team immediately appropriated the funds and purchased the new machine. The process improvement as measured by reject rate (decreased 20 percent), production speed (increased 48 percent), and lens quality ratings (increased 24 percent) was achieved within three months after purchasing the new equipment.

For most teams, the results of their process improvements are not quite as dramatic. In some cases, the improvements may be so subtle that they are difficult to measure. The key indicator of success is whether the process improvements meet the original customer requirements.

■ *Learning*. For many teams, the outcome of benchmarking is simply the opportunity to learn something new and bring new ideas into the organization. An IBM marketing manager started several benchmarking projects to understand state-of-the-art business applications. Although he and his team did not originally engage in the projects with any specific improvements in mind, they made dramatic changes in their business as a result of their benchmarking activities. He reported that the lack of project pressure made the benchmarking process all the more interesting and beneficial for him. This is a trend in many benchmarking efforts today. The benchmarkers are not simply out benchmarking, hoping to stumble across a new idea. On the contrary, they are dedicated to the concept of continuous improvement.

■ *Forming functional networks.* Some of the outcomes of the benchmarking process do not relate to the specific issue or problem that is being investigated, but have to do with some of the by-products of the benchmarking process. One of these added dimensions is the formation of functional benchmarking networks. As individuals participate in benchmarking activities on a continuous basis, they form a variety of professional contacts within their own organization, within their industry group, and possibly throughout the world. One individual benchmarker can have hundreds of benchmarking contacts. Once these networks are formed, the opportunities for "informal" benchmarking through one's network increase, and information can be canvassed, accumulated, and summarized in fairly short order.

The trend toward the formation of functional and industry group networks is increasing. Benchmarkers are realizing that they can sustain a continuous benchmarking process by simply keeping their networks active. As these networks grow in popularity, there will be greater opportunities for joint benchmarking projects cosponsored by large groups of organizations or by whole clusters of network members.

Recycling Efforts

Many of the formal benchmarking models in existence today include the basic direction to recycle or recalibrate. There are two implications to this directive. The first is to make adjustments in the benchmarking process itself—to examine the process during and after each benchmarking cycle in order to improve the fit between the benchmarking team and the process requirements. As individuals and teams gain experience and become proficient in their use of the process, they are able to diagnose their individual process strengths and weaknesses and adjust their benchmarking behaviors accordingly. For example, teams often find that after several iterations of the process, they become very efficient in Stages 1, 2, and 3. They are then able to allocate additional time and attention to Stage 4 (data collection and analysis). Another common adjustment is for the teams to shorten the anticipated time to complete a benchmarking project. Many organizations encourage their employees to engage in a process check during and after each benchmarking cycle. Such checks help individuals and teams maximize their benchmarking efficiency and effectiveness.

The second focus of recycling has to do with the continuous improvement of the work process itself. Given the basic assumption that functional best practices are a moving target, the search for emerging best-practices organizations and sources of new information and ideas is never-ending. Benchmarking is a continuous activity for those who want to maintain a state-of-the-art perspective. Most benchmarking teams emerge from the investigation process with many ideas and recycling possibilities. But benchmarking begins with a focus on specific critical success factors. The idea is to start with this specific information and work toward the broader concepts. As one explores these broader concepts (particularly in the process area), the exposure to new ideas and methods grows. Teams returning from site visits and interviews always have new ideas for improving their business and new ideas for benchmarking.

Seeing the Project Through

One of the problems with the benchmarking process (particularly when one is new to it) is that it is often time-consuming and requires a significant amount of project planning, team coordination, and, in some cases, travel time. This process often wears people out. After participation in a benchmarking project, there may be a project completion "high" followed by a postproject "low." Unfortunately, many people are too exhausted to spend quality time on the actual implementation of organizational improvements. This problem decreases as people gain more experience with the process and become more efficient at completing their assignments. As you begin to implement benchmarking in your organization, be careful that you don't fall into the trap of underestimating the amount of time and effort it will take to complete your first few cycles of the process.

As you complete your initial benchmarking cycles, it may be necessary to rally the members of the benchmarking team around a call to take action. Consider the process diagnostics that are listed in Exhibit 7-3. Whether you are producing a benchmarking report, communicating findings to others, implementing product or process improvements, or simply applying what you have learned to your own work, you have to generate enough energy to apply what you have learned and to continue to move ahead to identify other benchmarking opportunities.

Exhibit 7-3. The benchmarking process: Stage 5 diagnostics.

- ☐ You or your team has produced a report or summary of your benchmarking investigation. This summary conforms to any reporting format that has been established in your organization (e.g., on-line summary forms).

- ☐ The customers for your benchmarking investigation have received a review/report of your benchmarking investigation.

- ☐ You or your team has made an effort to capitalize on improvement outcomes:
    - Specific product/process improvements
    - Learning opportunities
    - Formation of functional networks

- ☐ You or your team encourages recycling efforts:
    - Improvement of the benchmarking process itself
    - Continuous improvement of the work product/process

Part Three

Recommendations From Best-Practices Benchmarkers

8

Ethical and Legal Issues

One of the most commonly asked questions in benchmarking seminars and training sessions has to do with the legal and ethical aspects of benchmarking. After receiving a basic briefing about the concept, many people anticipate all the potential problems associated with information transfer, particularly among competitors. The typical concerns and questions focus on a few common themes: antitrust, proprietary information, perspectives on competitive benchmarking, and the possibility of extensive interaction with corporate attorneys. Many people need to be convinced that the process works without "giving up the store," so to speak.

Most experienced benchmarking organizations have developed a legal and ethical position on the subject of benchmarking. The objective of this chapter is to review the recommendations of best-practices benchmarkers with respect to legal and ethical issues. Although these recommendations are by no means exhaustive, they do represent the perspective shared by most experienced benchmarking companies. As you begin the process of benchmarking, you will no doubt run into some of the issues presented here. Consider the following guidelines:

■ *Develop a formal position on ethical and legal issues.* Work with your legal staff to draft a general statement that identifies specific benchmarking topics, methodologies, and reporting protocols that are sensitive for your organization. If necessary, have your legal staff contact their counterparts in other organizations in order to increase their awareness of precedents or guidelines.

■ *Communicate your organization's position on legal and ethical issues.*

Once a formal position has been determined, it is vital that your organization communicate that information to any employee who might engage in benchmarking activity. This can usually be accomplished during the course of benchmarking training or briefing sessions. Companies such as Xerox, DEC, and IBM all touch on legal and ethical issues during their regular benchmarking training sessions. AT&T has developed a formal code of ethics that it makes available to every benchmarking team. In addition to communicating your legal and ethical position, you must also test for understanding to ensure that the message has reached the intended audience. One method of effectively communicating legal and ethical issues is to provide specific examples of behaviors and activities that illustrate and support the message.

■ *Clarify legal terms.* Many employees use words such as *proprietary* and *antitrust* without having any idea what these terms really mean or imply. The fact is that antitrust cases arising out of benchmarking activities are extremely rare. An excellent presentation on the subject of antitrust and proprietary information was delivered by a corporate attorney at a large oil company. During a presentation on the subject of benchmarking and competitive analysis, he drew a big square on a flipchart. He then drew a smaller square in one of the corners of the larger square—the smaller square taking approximately 20 percent of the area of the larger one. He stated that this smaller square represented, in his opinion, the amount of information that should be considered hands-off during benchmarking. He was quick to note that approximately 80 percent of the square was open, and he suggested that the organization loosen up with respect to its fears on the subject.

■ *Put all agreements in writing.* When you contact prospective benchmark partners, it is advisable to put all agreements regarding the benchmarking activity in writing. A good example of this type of document is a nondisclosure (or disclosure) agreement between the benchmarking organizations. These written agreements or statements of understanding should be kept on file for a period of at least two years. The written documents do not have to be drafted by attorneys, but it is advisable to have your legal staff recommend a format for those written statements.

■ *Clarify the need for legal review.* Most benchmarking investigations do not deal with proprietary information. In the majority of cases, there is no need for legal review of benchmarking topics. Your organization should clearly define any specific issues that might be subject to legal review prior to any formal information-collection activities.

Examples of Ethical and Legal Positions of Best-Practices Benchmarking Organizations

The following are excerpts from legal and ethical position statements of established benchmarking organizations. Most of these statements are part of these organizations' formal benchmarking training curricula.

■ *Information requests.* Never request information you would not give. This is the golden rule of benchmarking and is a common position among experienced benchmarking companies.

■ *Sensitive information.* Never benchmark sensitive or proprietary information with a competitor. In fact, sharing proprietary or sensitive information with anyone is discouraged. If benchmarking needs to be done with a competitor on a sensitive topic, engage the services of an independent consultant who will maintain the anonymity of the participants or will report information to those with a need to know only under the direction of the appropriate manager or management designate.

■ *Antitrust laws.* When obtaining benchmarking information, be aware of possible legal barriers. In certain instances, exchanging price or market share information with competitors may result in a violation of the Sherman Antitrust Act, which attempts to prevent price-fixing among the market's major competitors while trying to avoid restraint of trade. If you are operating in a market with few competitors and you discuss price with those competitors, you could be accused of sharing price information. In turn, courts could cite you for price-fixing.

The basic message that should be communicated to all employees who might engage in data-gathering activities is to exercise caution when discussing any sensitive areas such as price, market share, and technologies with major competitors. This caution is particularly relevant if you conduct business in a market that is dominated by a relatively small number of organizations.

■ *Confidentiality.* Never talk about another company without its permission. That is, treat all information you hear as confidential. Get approvals in writing before you quote another source or use a story from another organization to illustrate a point.

■ *Job interviews.* Candidates like to impress recruiters, and it is unacceptable to take advantage of the situation by enticing candidates to divulge nonpublic information, even if the candidate is not deliberately revealing secrets and is not being forced or influenced to do so. State that you do not want any information that would be considered confidential by the candidate's employer.

■ *Hiring from competitors.* Individuals can be hired for their skills and abilities, but they cannot be hired for the confidential competitive information they possess.

■ *Trade shows and conferences.* Employees cannot misrepresent themselves while gathering information at these types of events. Employees do not need to reveal their identity if the information they are gathering is furnished to all attendees, for example, at a competitor's display booth. However, employees should reveal their organizational identity and purpose if the information they are seeking is not public.

■ *Management consultants.* It is inappropriate to use consultants to gather information under any type of false or misleading pretenses, such as hiring a consultant to perform an "independent" study of a market and provide information to you that is not available to other participants in the data-collection effort.

■ *Phony bids.* It is illegal to ask a customer to solicit requests for proposals from your competitors and ask information regarding parts, technology, price, and so on.

■ *Suppliers.* It is generally acceptable to check the output of another organization by asking its supplier about volumes of key parts shipped. However, it is unacceptable to entice a supplier to divulge information by suggesting that you will use its services only in exchange for information regarding your competitors or other companies.

■ *Internal telephone books and organizational charts.* It is unacceptable to obtain such internal documents by misrepresentation.

■ *Plant tours.* If tours are not open to the public, reveal the identity of your organization and the purpose of your interest in a tour.

■ *Reverse engineering.* This practice of product dismantling or deconstruction is acceptable only if a product or service is obtained legally.

■ *Awareness of organizational level.* Don't knowingly take advantage of lower-level employees by getting them to disclose information that they might not know will harm their organization. Make an effort to contact someone at the manager level or above.

■ *Taking advantage of personal relationships.* Often employees from other organizations are uncomfortable about discussing certain information with you, especially when they think it may be proprietary. No matter how friendly you are with certain individuals in another company, never ask them to reveal information as a "personal favor."

■ *Full disclosure.* Make sure you always identify yourself, your organization, and your purpose to your benchmark partners. Clearly state your purpose. Never misrepresent yourself or provide misleading information about your intentions.

Developing Your Own Code of Ethics

As you begin to plan for the launch of your benchmarking activities, consider drafting your own organizational benchmarking code of ethics. This code should be practical and reasonable given the scope and intent of your organization's benchmarking objectives. A benchmarker at AT&T suggested that an interesting assignment for a pilot benchmarking team would be to benchmark the legal and ethical issues and policies of a variety of best-practices benchmarking companies. The team would then be responsible for developing its own code of ethics that could be adopted by the organization as an official guide.

A formal statement of ethics can serve as an effective message of intent to your benchmark partners. As you prepare to make formal contact with prospective partners, consider including a statement of ethics as part of your overall project package. The inclusion of such a statement might encourage organizations to participate in your benchmarking efforts. A strong statement of ethics or values can make a strong impact on people who do not fully understand or appreciate the intent of the benchmarking process.

9

Keys to Benchmarking Success

The review of the benchmarking process presented in this book has provided you with the basic guidelines you need to plan and conduct a benchmarking investigation. The benchmarking process is neither complicated nor difficult to implement. But the question remains: Why are there so many benchmarking false starts and disappointments? Most problems are due to a lack of process discipline and an effort to manage the process according to traditional rules and paradigms. I feel sorry for trainees who attend benchmarking seminars and lament the fact that their bosses have instructed them to conduct a benchmarking investigation and have it completed by the end of the month. Only someone who has never been a member of a benchmarking team or managed a benchmarking investigation could make such an unreasonable request.

On the positive side, there are more excellent opportunities to benchmark today than there have ever been, and the outlook for the next several years is encouraging. Benchmarking networks and consortia are being formed almost daily. Benchmarking conferences and symposia are providing a place for benchmarkers to gather and strengthen their personal and organizational networks. Publications are beginning to focus on the issue of benchmarking, and they are providing excellent leads and ideas for those interested in starting the process or improving their existing benchmarking activities.

What the Future Holds

As I talked about the future of benchmarking with twenty-four of the best-practices benchmarking companies, several concepts emerged as the factors that would sustain the development of the benchmarking process and allow these organizations to take better advantage of their process capabilities. The following items were identified as areas of improvement and opportunity:

- The development of more professional, functional, and industry consortia and the ensuing opportunities to network among experienced benchmarkers.
- A need to educate prospective benchmarkers on proper methodology and basic process discipline. As information needs increase, best-practices organizations will demand more from their partners in terms of preparation and professionalism.
- Better use of internal on-line systems to track benchmarking projects and network information, and development of better software support tools.
- Additional efforts to remove process inefficiencies and encourage increased process discipline, along with improved quantity and quality of expert process facilitation.
- Additional pressures for return on investment (ROI) analysis on some benchmarking projects.
- More intense efforts to make the process recycle effectively— more follow-up on completed projects.
- Increased emphasis on coordination of benchmarking efforts among internal benchmarkers, especially in multidivisional and international organizations.
- The development of specialty newsletters (paper and on-line) dedicated to benchmarking activities.
- Improved quality and quantity of basic benchmarking training.
- Better integration with existing tools, processes, and programs.
- More of a trend to make benchmarking a way of life.

Advice From the Best

The best-practices benchmarking companies were asked to summarize some basic recommendations for organizations that are in the start-up phases of benchmarking. Many of these recommendations were consistent and deserve consideration from novice benchmarkers.

1. *Seek change and be action-oriented.* Benchmarking is not a passive

exercise. It is not a process well suited to those who are fishing for ideas or have not made up their minds about their desire to change. Benchmarking information supports action—it is in the context of planned change that the process has the most value.

2. *Be open to new ideas*. Benchmarking is a seeking out of new ideas. It is an attempt to stimulate an organization "out of the box" that it is in. If you tend to rationalize, justify, or deny in the presence of new ideas or alternative ways of doing things, benchmarking may not be for you.

3. *Know yourself before you attempt to know others*. Benchmarking begins with a thorough understanding of your own organizational products and processes. In most cases, benchmarking the activities of others when you don't understand yourself is a waste of time. If you are going to compare yourself with someone else, you had better have a good sense of your own performance first.

4. *Focus on the improvement of practices*. Don't focus on the measurement of operations and don't fixate on the numbers. Maintain a process focus rather than an object focus. Things tend to be static, while processes tend to be dynamic.

5. *Introduce and maintain discipline*. Structure your benchmarking process and provide adequate facilitation to benchmarking teams. Beware of process shortcuts early in the benchmarking process—a sure indication of shortcuts to come and possible process failure.

6. *Put the resources in place to get the job done right*:

- Get senior managers involved in the process. Discourage commissioned benchmarking studies from senior staff without a commitment to change or action.
- Make sure that you have allowed sufficient time to do the job right.
- Ensure that funding is budgeted for next year's benchmarking activities.
- Involve your best and brightest people in the process.
- Reward those who participate in the process.
- Ensure that your organization provides adequate communications about the benchmarking process, its intent, uses, and results.

Index